SCARED TO LIFE

The 1995 Chapel of the Air 50-Day Spiritual Adventure "Facing Down Our Fears"

Scared to Life, by Douglas J. Rumford. Discover how to break free of the gravitational pull of fear and its draining power by relying on God's resources. Book includes group discussion questions. Catalog no. 6-3413.

How to Fear God Without Being Afraid of Him, by David New and Randy Petersen. Do you have an unhealthy fear of God? This book will help you better understand God's power and holiness, balanced with His great love and care for each of His children. Catalog no. 6-3414. Audio book also available, Catalog no. 3-1228.

Adventure Journals. Dig deeper into the Adventure with day-by-day personal growth exercises. Available in the following editions:

Adult	Catalog no. 6-8870
Student	Catalog no. 6-8868
Children, grades 3–6	Catalog no. 6-8867
Critter County Activity Book (K–2)	Catalog no. 6-8866

ALSO AVAILABLE

Church Starter Kit	Catalog no. 6-8879
Children's Church Leader's Guide	Catalog no. 6-8865
Small Group Starter Kit	Catalog no. 6-8871
Student Leader's Guide	Catalog no. 6-8869

Contact your local Christian bookstore for still other 1995 Adventure products.

SCARED TO LIFE

DOUGLAS J. RUMFORD

VICTOR BOOKS

A DIVISION OF SCRIPTURE PRESS PUBLICATIONS INC.
USA CANADA ENGLAND

Copyediting: Barbara Williams

Cover Design: Scott Rattray

Cover Illustration: Tony Stone Worldwide

Rumford, Douglas.
    Scared to life / by Douglas Rumford.
    p.   cm.
    Includes bibliographical references.
    ISBN   1-56476-413-3
    1. Anxiety—Religious aspects—Christianity.   2. Fear—Religious aspects—
Christianity. 3. Christian life.   I. Title.
BV4908.5.R86   1994
248.8′6—dc20   94-29603
                                                                     CIP

2   3   4   5   6   7   8   9   10   Printing / Year   98   97   96   95   94

Published in association with the literary agency of Alive Communications,
P.O. Box 49068, Colorado Springs, Colorado 80949.

Dedicated to

My wife, Sarah,
A woman of courage, faith, and love
who has won my heart.

And to our children
Kristen Joy
Matthew Douglas
Timothy Andrew
Peter Jonathan

May the glorious grace and truth of Jesus Christ be written
on your hearts and flow joyfully from your lives
by the Spirit of the Living God.

I love you!

Glory To God

CONTENTS

Foreword

"Facing Down Our Fears." That was the topic a group of pastors proposed for our newest 50-Day Spiritual Adventure. I remember my initial response. "Someone else is going to have to write the key book this year," I stated almost immediately. "Fear is not something I've experienced that much. In fact, I can hardly remember being afraid about anything!" Little did I know that during the next several months a series of events would take place, causing me to experience fear in a way I never thought possible.

Every time a new Spiritual Adventure is announced, my staff kind of groans. "Now we'll have to live with this topic for a while," they say, "to make sure what we tell people is authentic." It seems that's been the story of our yearly Adventures. Maybe the authenticity factor is what makes these times of accelerated spiritual growth so popular.

A year ago, when I was still naive as to fear, I prayed about who should write the book that would be used during the Adventure. Actually, that was kind of a fearful decision in itself. I wasn't sure I wanted to give away something that I had always taken care of. But I did feel strongly led of the Lord to contact Dr. Doug Rumford. Now that I've read his completed manuscript, I know this was a valid sense of God's leading.

Doug has handled all of the fear-related topics both biblically and masterfully. With genuine empathy for those who find these fears troublesome, he makes the real excitement of his book showing us how God can do something marvelous in lives even in the face of such fears.

I like his title, *Scared to Life*.

I've heard that courage is becoming a lost quality in the church. If that's true, it's time to work on bringing it back. I know my spirit resonates with the challenge of being more courageous in my faith. As God speaks to you through these pages, I expect you will respond in the same way.

Fear in this society is not going to go away. Rather, it will become an ever-increasing part of our culture. Now is the time to begin allowing Christ to demonstrate in us the same bravery He showed while here on earth. To me it all sounds exciting!

David Mains, Director
The Chapel of the Air Ministries

Acknowledgments

My deepest thanks to David Mains and the Chapel of the Air. You are one of the most encouraging and innovative ministries of "revitalizing Christians and their churches." Thanks also to David New, Marian Oliver, and the rest of the Chapel team for taking a chance on me. I dared to dream again, and you helped it come true!

To Greg Clouse, Barbara Williams, and the editorial staff of Victor Books, I want to express my deepest appreciation for your affirmation and support throughout this whole process.

To the staff of First Presbyterian Church, Fresno, California: Dr. Ernie Bradley, Dr. Julie Carter, Lydia Contreras, the Rev. Wayne Eberly, Susan Glover, Terry Haley, Judy Hulstrom, Sue Cavallini, Donna Rayburn, the Rev. Chuck Shillito, and John Wedwick. Thank you for cheering me on and for enduring with good humor and practical help the additional demands which resulted from my writing.

A special thanks to my secretary, Tess Mott, whose joyful spirit and ability have made "lighter work" of this project.

To the elders and congregation of First Presbyterian Church, Fresno, California, who have taught me much about the courage of faith. You have encouraged me as together we seek to serve the Lord to the fullest of our abilities. Thank you for your prayers and for allowing me to share some of your stories.

To Stuart Conrad and Bobbye Temple who read and commented on the final draft as the deadline loomed large. Thank you for your flexibility, insight, and thoughtful review.

To Greg Johnson, my agent with Alive Communications, Inc., for his guidance and editorial skill.

To my family, to whom this book is dedicated. I'm back!

An Invitation to Faith-powered Living

"Hold it right there! I've got you in my night-scope!"

Jack and I looked at each other in stunned amazement.

"Don't move—or I'll blow you away!"

Moments earlier Jack and I had been walking down a deserted country road cut into a hillside in rural Indiana. We had brought the junior high youth from our church here for a retreat. Now, some other sponsors were with them, so we could take a break. We were enjoying the bright light of stars we usually couldn't see living in the city. The quiet crunch of gravel under our shoes joined the chorus of crickets as we got caught up in conversation. When we came around a bend, we suddenly heard the sound of a racing car and saw a set of headlights weaving back and forth across the road. The speeding car was coming our way, so we jumped off the road to lie along the hillside. The car sped past us, went around another bend, and stopped. We heard doors open and close, people shouting—though we couldn't understand what they were saying—and then the car turned around and flew past us, as we still lay on the hillside. We must have stayed where we were for about fifteen minutes, then we decided there was no problem continuing our walk. It was such a beautiful early summer night.

"Hold it right there! I've got you in my night-scope!"

I reached up to scratch my ear.

"Don't move—or I'll blow you away!"

I could not believe what was happening.

"You know what a night-scope is?" said a voice from above us on the hill. Without waiting for our answer, he went on to explain, "It takes all the light from the stars and magnifies it so I can see you two as plain as in the sunlight."

"Dear Jesus, keep us safe," I heard Jack whisper.

"Amen!" I whispered.

Then we heard the cracking of underbrush and sliding of rocks and dirt as our assailant came down the hillside toward us.

"What are you boys doing here? Nobody walks around here late at night. I don't think you belong here. . . ."

As he spoke, I felt as if I were living through a movie or a dream. It just couldn't be real.

The man then jumped onto the road in front of us, let out a shout, spun around, and fell flat on his back. There didn't seem to be anything in his hands—then I saw a glint of light! He wasn't moving, so we edged closer, closer, closer . . . finally we could see it—the glint of a bottle!

The rush of relief mingled with the churning of anxiety and anger made us both nearly hysterical with laughter. As we alternately thanked the Lord for delivering us and wondered what to do with this drunken man, we noticed a light at the top of the hill. It was a house. A woman and younger man came out and were walking down a driveway toward us, apparently family members. We helped them get the man up to the house. They apologized, and we said good night, heading back to the peace and quiet of our junior high retreat.

I still remember how that first icy touch of fear made me feel. Life became vivid. I guess the intensity is what made it so dreamlike. All systems were put on full alert. Later, when Jack and I discussed how we felt, we learned that we had both been calculating how we could escape, bobbing and weaving down the hill. We both felt a peace in the midst of the panic. There was an excitement and drama we had never felt before, but we would never want it again!

Fear in a crisis is understandable. It serves an essential function: alerting us to the possibility of danger or threat and preparing us to respond appropriately. The problem arises when fear moves from being an alarm that alerts us to an anxiety that controls us. To live daily under the tyranny of fear erodes all aspects of life.

Inscribed across an old map of Jamaica is the phrase, "The Land of Look Behind." It was drawn in the days when escaping slaves would flee from the lowlands into the mountains. Since the government would send troops after the escaping slaves, the runaways would look fearfully over their shoulders, dreading to catch a glimpse of the pursuing army. Thus the mountains came to be called, "The Land of Look Behind."[1]

Many of us spend much of our lives in the Land of Look Behind. We are looking over our shoulders, spooked by the fears of life. It began at an early age. Remember some of your childhood fears?

Running up the stairs from the dark basement—I was certain I could feel the "thing" clutching at my heels!

Throwing a snowball at a car, then hearing the car screech to a halt and begin to back up; "Dear God, get me out of this, and I'll never throw a snowball again!"

Making that first-ever phone call to a girl I had a crush on; I'm sure her parents called the phone company: "Yes, could you help us? Our phone keeps ringing, but there's no one there when we pick it up. . . ."

Making my first, and my hundred-and-first, evangelism visit! I thought when the Lord talked about knocking, He was referring to doors—but I think it relates better to knees!

Fear is a fact of life. Fears change as we grow, but fear doesn't go away. Many of us, however, have become so used to fear that we hardly notice its corrosive influence on our daily lives. Take a moment and inventory your own experience:

> How much of what you do each day is motivated by fear? Are you driven by fear of losing a job? Fear of failing in school? Fear of not pleasing people? Fear of getting caught for something you did that was wrong?

> How many of your relationships have significant "fear factors"? Fear factors include being afraid to be honest, afraid to confront, afraid to say no, afraid to disagree.

> What portion of your financial resources are allocated out of fear? How much is invested in a home security system? How much of our tax dollars are directed by fear?

Fear is one of the main motivators of life, right up there with guilt. It works too—for a time. But it exacts a high price. Whether we motivate ourselves or others by fear, the end result leaves us less than when we started. We may perform and achieve goals, but they will not be enjoyed as fully as they would had they been attained in a life-affirming manner. Achievement based on fear will always smell of the musty odors of anxiety and resentment.

Fear is also present in many relationships. Have you ever found yourself going to a friend with a problem concerning someone you both know? Why not go directly to the person with whom you have the problem? Honestly, it is usually because we are afraid of how he will respond, or afraid that she may say things that will hurt us. It happens in the workplace, the church committee, the school, the charity organization, and the family. How many poor decisions can be traced to the inability to overcome this fear? Fear makes us trade robust relationships which thrive on "speaking the truth in love" for fragile friendships built on shallow clichés and the avoidance of difficult conversations.

Fear is good business. In the United States, cashing in on

fear is reaching entrepreneurial proportions! The home and automobile security industries have grown exponentially over the last decade. The newest trend in housing is the "gate-guarded development." These housing communities are walled, allowing access only through a manned security station or electronic gate. While many think of this as progress, we need to ask ourselves whether or not we are returning to the Middle Ages when the protection of walls was necessary for survival. One of the most impressive signs of social progress emerging from the Middle Ages was the disappearance of the walled city. Now, the walls are rising again.

Fear is real. There is no doubt that many threats are valid. The purpose of this book is not to try to rid us of our fear reflex. It is essential to our survival. The real issues are these: First, to what extent are we leading fear-driven lives, always looking over our shoulders? Second, how can we learn to lead faith-powered lives?

We will explore a number of specific principles for facing down our fears, but two axioms are foundational. First, the fundamental nature of fear is spiritual. While there are many physical threats which confront us, and many practical actions we can take to oppose them, both the headwaters of fear and the wellsprings of hope are spiritual. In his second letter to Timothy, the Apostle Paul writes, "For God did not give us a spirit of timidity, but a spirit of power, of love and of self-discipline" (2 Tim. 1:7). Timidity is a type of fear characteristic of our old nature. The strategy for awakening faith in the face of fear is to learn to draw on the Holy Spirit indwelling us with power, love, and self-discipline. These three resources are our anchors holding us firm against the overwhelming floods of life.

The spirit of power provides a reality check against the deception that fear can overwhelm us. We remind ourselves that, in spite of appearances, "the one who is in [us] is greater than the one who is in the world" (1 John 4:4). It may not seem so at the time, but it is true and will become apparent. We must not be simplistic about this, but we must nurture this confidence.

The spirit of love provides our guiding principle in all relationships. A consistent strategy of love guards us from the worldly temptations that arise from the anxiety of fear. We seek the way of love: tough love when necessary. Tough love is love which reinforces the responsibility and respect of all people in the relationships, as opposed to the seduction of rescuing or excusing destructive behavior and the violation of personal boundaries.

Self-discipline is an essential aspect of our dignity as followers of Jesus. It is also one of the prime targets of the enemy. When we face our fears, our dignity grows and our sense of appropriate personal power grows. The discipline of self-control speaks to the development of character that is to mark our lives as we walk through the valley of the shadows. As redeemed children of the King, this principle affirms the power God has placed within us as people created in His image and redeemed by His love in Christ.

We must see behind fear's disguises. The wise observation that "love drives out fear" (1 John 4:18) is derived from understanding the spiritual roots of fear. The antidote to fear is love. The only adequate source of love is that revealed in Jesus Christ. To know victory over fear, we will want to know the Lord who says, "Fear not."

The second axiom for confronting fear is that the primary strategy for awakening faith and courage comes from renewing our minds, reshaping our assumptions, and responding according to the principles revealed in God's Word. Our struggles with fear are often fought on the battlefield of the mind long before they touch other aspects of our lives. Therefore, we need to take time to analyze the dynamics of fear and develop the principles of Scripture to "take captive every thought to make it obedient to Christ" (2 Cor. 10:5).

The first and most productive line of defense is to examine our fears in the light of truth. Then, we can replace fear and doubt with knowledge and action. The importance of right thinking is illustrated by Denis Waitley in his book, *Seeds of Greatness.* Waitley defines fear as "F.E.A.R.—*False Education Appearing Real.*"[2] Our minds can turn against us if we allow false concepts to take root. This "false education" may be formal or informal, but it does not match with the reality of things as they are. For example, we may think that we could never make a difference in turning the tide of crime in our neighborhood, town, or city. The truth is, however, that many individuals and small groups are tackling this problem and are making a big difference. Or, we may think there is no hope for our forgiveness because we've done "the worst thing." We are blinded to God's truth by our guilt and shame. In this case, we need to banish falsehood with God's Word which says, "If we confess our sins, He is faithful and just and will forgive us our sins, and purify us from all unrighteousness. If we claim we have not sinned, we make Him out to be a liar and His word has no place in our lives" (1 John 1:9-10).

Waitley cites a University of Michigan study[3] which determined that:

> 60% of our fears are totally unwarranted;
> 20% have already become past activities and are out of our control;
> 10% are so petty that they do not make any difference at all;
> 4–5% of the remaining 10% are real and justifiable, but we cannot do anything about them:
> This means that approximately 5% of our fears are real fears that we can do something about.

Too much of our energy pours down the drain of anxious worry and fear, when it could be channeled to turn the turbines of productive change and joyful living. The waste must stop!

The purpose of this book is to awaken us to faith-powered living in a time when most lives are driven by fear. A faith-powered life begins as we become aware of fear's foothold in our lives. Time spent getting to know ourselves is one of the most productive first steps to interrupting the unconscious fear-cycles that hamper us.

The second step to leading a faith-powered life is to develop both a biblical perspective on the threats of life and an inventory of biblical resources to meet those threats. God's Word is a practical manual for facing our fears. We learn to understand the true nature of fear and the true source of power we need to overcome it. As the psalmist wrote,

> The Lord is my light and my salvation—
> whom shall I fear?
> The Lord is the stronghold of my life—
> of whom shall I be afraid?
>
> (Ps. 27:1)

The third step to continue in faith-powered living is to train ourselves to use a repertoire of faith-rooted responses. We need to equip ourselves with principles that channel the flood tides of fear into energy that can sweep away the fear sources.

The most productive use of this material is in its stimulation of your own reflection on the forces of fear and the abundant resources of faith in your own life. You will grow most not from the insights of these pages, but from those the Holy Spirit will impress on your heart through reading these words, and above all, through reading God's Word. To encourage this process of personally encountering the fear issues in your life, each chapter concludes with a section I have called "Investing in Your R & D." Any business knows that progress requires heavy investment in "R & D," short for "Research and Development." Genuine change requires reflection that can help you translate insight into experience. By "R & D," I mean "Reflection and Discussion." These materials will suggest ways you can research your own experience and God's truth so that you can move toward change. My hope is that we will find that our fears are not meant to scare us to death; they can scare us to life!

1. What things do you do each day that are motivated by fear?

2. Which of the following areas present the most concern to you? You might want to put them in "rank order," from most fearful (designated as #1) to least fearful.
___ a. Fear of losing a job?
___ b. Fear of failing in school?
_2_ c. Fear of not pleasing people?
___ d. Fear of getting caught for something you did that you know was wrong?
_1_ e. Fear of something happening to someone you love?
_5_ f. Fear of becoming a victim of crime?
_4_ g. Fear of a natural catastrophe?
_3_ h. Fear of not being loved by a spouse, parent, family member, or close friend?
___ i. Other_____

3. How would you describe your primary way(s) of coping with fear?

4. How would you like to change your coping strategy?

5. In light of the University of Michigan study, take a few moments to brainstorm the fears you are wrestling with at this time.
   a. What "60 percent Fears" are part of the totally unwarranted fears, having a very, very slim chance of affecting you?
   b. What "20 percent Fears" do you have concerning things that are past or beyond your control?
   c. What "10 percent Fears" are, in all honesty, so petty that they do not make any difference at all?
   d. What are your "You-Just-Gotta-Live-with-It Fears"? This refers to the 4–5 percent of the remaining 10 percent of your fears that are real and justifiable, but you cannot do anything about them.

e. What "Final 5 percent Fears" are real fears that you may in fact be able to do something about? Which of these would you prefer to resolve first?

6. In what ways have you found fear-factors to be an issue in your relationships? How have you had success confronting some of these fears? What do you need to help you improve?

7. In what ways has fear been a drain on your resources (financial, emotional, spiritual, relational)? What would you be able to do if you could invest less in "fear stocks" and invest more in "faith stock"?

Chapter One

Shaken to Our Senses

Much of fear's power lies in the unknown. Our confidence is most easily shaken, not by that which we know, but by that which we do not know. The hardest part of confronting an illness is waiting until the problem is diagnosed. As we languish in uncertainty, we often prepare ourselves for the worst, visualizing many things we would be embarrassed to admit. This dynamic of fear percolates through all aspects of life. More than a few people are intimidated by the fear of entering an unknown situation, meeting new people, or traveling to new places. Our imaginative powers sabotage our confidence with "what if...?" images of discomfort, distress, and catastrophe.

We are living in an era which is marked by the unknown. The acceleration of change is shaking the confidence of many people. The rate of technological change has increased exponentially while the rate of human adaptation seems to have peaked and begun to decline. We are overloaded, suffering in record numbers with stress and anxiety disorders. Likewise, the rate of change in world politics has shaken our security. We are learning that a world which is more free is not necessarily more safe. The euphoria which accompanied the fall of the Berlin Wall in 1989 has been smothered by the rise of many other obstacles to peace. The end of the Cold War standoff between the free world and the Communist Bloc has not brought the world closer to peace. Instead, we have traded a relatively predictable bilateral threat for a chaotic multilateral threat of far more disconcerting proportions. It's as if a mother spider were killed and thousands of babies scattered in every direction, spinning their webs of terror.

We are facing a shift like that which confronted the British soldiers during the Revolutionary War in America in 1776. They suffered staggering casualties because they wore bright red coats and fought in disciplined ranks, while they faced the "unorthodox" rebels of the new world who wore nondescript clothing and fought from behind trees. The British failure to develop new strategies to confront new threats was a significant reason why they lost the new world. We too must develop new strategies to confront our new fears, or risk losing the promise of the new world that is replacing the world as we've known it. The world as we have known it is fading away. The unknown is upon us. How will we cope?

When we're overwhelmed with the unknown, we need to cling to the known, to that which is unchanging. It's much like coping with motion sickness. Have you ever wondered why the driver of a car rarely gets sick, though that same person may find themselves overcome by nausea if he rides in the back seat? Extensive research studies have concluded that the nausea of motion sickness comes from "slippage of the eyes." Our equilibrium is closely associated with our optic sense. When we are moving, especially at a high rate of speed, or with continual twisting and turning, our eyes may have difficulty adjusting to the erratic bumps and bounces of the vehicle's continual motion. They slip from focal points and upset our equilibrium. The remedy? Look to the far horizon—to that which is not moving and shifting. The reason the driver of a car usually does not suffer motion sickness is because she continually looks ahead. Her eyes rest frequently on the still point, enabling them to handle the other jostles and jolts.

This is a model for turbulent times. Our equilibrium is shaken as we are moving through life too quickly, twisting and turning to confront demands that are pressing too closely. We are nauseated by the continual motion of life. A "slippage of our spiritual sight" occurs when we fail to maintain our focus on the Lord. Fear gains a foothold, and faith fades in strength. The only hope is to lift our eyes to the far horizon of faith.

Finding Your Horizon Point

Isaiah, whom we now call a prophet, knew what it was to face a crisis of fear in uncertain times. He had been leading a satisfying, stable life during a golden age in Judah. He had become a scribe in the royal palace in Jerusalem during the reign of King Uzziah (also called Azariah). Uzziah had ruled Judah for fifty-two years. Only one king, Manasseh, had ruled longer. Uzziah's long, prosperous reign was marked by tremendous success in every aspect of national life. He was victorious over the Philistine menace, breaking into their fortifications and establishing prosperous settlements in their territory. He fortified Jerusalem and developed a powerful army which no surrounding nation could withstand. He expanded agricultural prosperity for those with cattle and those with farms and vineyards. And "his fame spread far and wide, for he was greatly helped until he became powerful" (2 Chron. 26:15).

As often happens, the seeds of destruction germinate in times of prosperity. Uzziah's success led to his downfall. Pride and presumption seduced him into assuming the role of priest and offering incense in the temple. In the nation of Judah, there were strictly delineated roles for the prophet, the priest, and the king. The king was to be subservient to the priest and the prophet. This was to reflect the fact that God was still the primary ruler of the people. Uzziah's refusal to heed the rebuke of the priest (also named Azariah!) brought judgment on him. A leprous disease broke out on his forehead, leading to his exclusion from the public life and worship of the nation. Uzziah learned one of the saddest ironies of life: when pride seduces us, it then separates us from what we most value.

The nation continued on the inertia of prosperity for a time, but then began to lose momentum. Without the energy of faith and faithfulness that had characterized Uzziah's initial reign (vv. 4-5), the people became vulnerable to threats from within and from the outside. Upon Uzziah's death, Judah was forced to struggle for survival against the alliance formed by

Pekah of the Northern Kingdom of Israel and Rezin of Damascus. The pressures continued to mount as Judah slid into decline.

In desperation, Isaiah sought his horizon point: "In the year that King Uzziah died, I saw the Lord seated on a throne" (Isa. 6:1). In the year that King Uzziah died, the nation's dreams were dealt a life-threatening blow. They were entering a time of treacherous transition, when anything could happen. Though change was inevitable, few were prepared for the adjustments it would demand, for the assumptions it would challenge, for the cost it would exact. Isaiah, however, was prepared to take the essential first step. His reflex in fear was to turn to his faith. He considered the temple, that still point in a world spinning out of control. As he turned from the "empty" throne of Judah—vacated by the only ruler Isaiah had ever known—he found the One who is always on His throne.[1]

Fear, properly understood and managed, can clarify our vision. We would be foolish to deny the messages that come to us through fear. We nurture spiritual health when we openly acknowledge the reality of our fear, but learn how to respond intentionally to it. We need to be honest about fear's threat, but move through it to faith's promise of courage. When we do so, fear serves as an alarm which awakens us to faith and action rather than as a force which renders us helpless.

Take a moment and reflect on the fears that touch your daily life. What sort of fears do you wrestle with? Fear of what people will think, fear of becoming a victim of crime, fear of your financial or career security, fear of your parents' welfare as they are aging, fear of your children's welfare? Many more could be listed. These fears are alerting you to genuine issues that need your attention. They are meant to be alarms, awakening you to action, not forces which bind you in anxious paralysis.

Isaiah's experience reveals how fear can awaken faith. First, fear can awaken faith when we use it as a mirror of our souls. Our fear reflects our inner state of being. We ask ourselves, "Fear, why are you here?" When we feel the nausea of fear rising within, we know that our vision is fixed too low. We need to look up from the jostling situation to the horizon of hope. For Isaiah, this meant looking to the Lord. For us, it means looking to the Lord, especially by turning to Scripture. Our horizon is the Word of God.

God's Word provides solid confidence when all around us is shaking. The psalmist sang:

> God is our refuge and strength,
>   an ever-present help in trouble.
> Therefore we will not fear, though the earth give way,
>   and the mountains fall into the heart of the sea.
>   (Ps. 46:1-2)

I have spoken with many friends who have experienced severe earthquakes in Southern California. They have said they have never experienced anything as frightening and unsettling as a powerful earthquake. When the earth is shaking, there is nowhere to go. You cannot run away because everywhere is affected. The psalmist, however, who must have had experience with earthquakes, found his horizon point in the unmovable faithfulness of God.

Among other truths, the Bible tells us to expect the crumbling of society apart from the Lord. The Bible teaches us to expect the worst from the world. This is not a call to pessimism. Rather, there is a biblical realism that gives stability. When we are shocked by the events of life, we are revealing our inability to accept God's clear teaching concerning the depth of human depravity and the extent of sin's curse on this fallen world. We live in a type of denial. When the Lord pronounced the curses in Genesis 3, He was laying out a new set of expectations for the world. Life is not only difficult, it is impossible. This world is doomed apart from the intervention of God.

After describing the persecution and trials His followers would suffer, Jesus said, "I have told you these things, so that in Me you may have peace. In this world you will have trouble. But take heart! I have overcome the world" (John 16:33). It's as if Jesus were saying, "When problems come, you're going to think I've left you. I want to tell you that when problems come, it's the sign that I'm with you. Learn to use your trials as triggers to faith."

When we are tempted to take trouble as a sign that God has forsaken us, Jesus teaches us to take it as a sign that God has prepared us. He has already warned us that we are citizens of a new kingdom, living behind enemy lines. We live under enemy fire. As such, we will suffer for at least two reasons. First, we will suffer by virtue of being human, as all others suffer (see Rom. 8:18-21). The created order has not been fully redeemed. As human creatures with mortal bodies, we will face fearful circumstances. Second, we will also suffer as followers of Jesus Christ. We will come under attack from the world, the flesh, and the devil. When we fix our eyes on the Lord, resting them on the horizon point of faith, the soul sickness of fear subsides and our strength and courage rise.

In the midst of the Civil War, a friend of Abraham Lincoln's was staying at the White House. This visitor was unable to sleep. He heard the sound of a voice coming from the President's bedroom. He wandered in and saw the President kneeling before an open Bible. "His back was toward me," the visitor wrote, "I shall never forget his prayer. 'O Thou God that heard Solomon in the night when he prayed and cried for wisdom, hear me . . . I cannot guide the affairs of this nation without Thy help. Hear me and save this nation.' "[2]

Whether presidents or ordinary people, we find ourselves facing situations that tax us to the limit, and then some. Our habit of heart needs to be prayer, fixed on the horizon of faith, not panic.

Seeing Life from the Eternal Perspective

When Isaiah stopped to look to the Lord, he started to see both the Lord and his own life in a new way. He saw a vision of the Lord, "high and exalted, and the train of His robe filled the temple" (Isa. 6:1). It's important to note that Isaiah received this vision of the Lord before he had done anything to merit such a gift. We see here the expression of grace. Isaiah was overwhelmed by the desperation of his nation. He had nothing to offer God except a sacrifice of tears. Such is the sacrifice God accepts. When we turn to Him, He will reveal Himself to us.

We need not, indeed we must not, be so ashamed of our fear that we try to hide it from God and ourselves. When we turn to Him in our fear, He comes to us with Himself as our chief comfort. God did not give Isaiah a plan for action, nor a lecture on the evils of the society. Instead, God gave Himself—and everything else that was necessary followed in its proper time.

This is the second key to awakening courageous faith in a time of fear: Faith awakens as our vision of God's glory grows. Isaiah saw "the Lord seated on the throne." Earthly kings come and go, but the Sovereign Lord reigns on. When our confidence is grounded in eternity, it is not easily uprooted by the winds of crisis.

The praise of the seraphs also quickened the pulse of flagging faith. One of the characteristics of the Hebrew language is the use of repetition to communicate emphasis.[3] Hebrew does not have the varied punctuation marks that English has. It does not have the exclamation point which English uses to emphasize an idea. When a Hebrew wanted to underline a point, the person repeated it. Jesus did this when He wanted to teach an important lesson on priorities: "Martha, Martha; you are worried and upset about many things, but only one thing is needed" (Luke 10:41-42). The standard repetition was two times, as in Jesus' repetition of "Martha, Martha."

The threefold repetition of "Holy, holy, holy" in Isaiah emphasizes the infinite holiness of God. We usually think of the word "holy" in moral terms, meaning "without sin or imperfection." This term, however, is not limited to a moral description. Literally, to "be holy" means "to be separate from." It is a category of existence which means living apart from the control of the world, apart from the power of human circumstances. "Holy" describes the separateness and sovereignty of God apart from the circumstances of life which gives us confidence that He can overcome those circumstances. God is not enmeshed in the cause-and-effect dynamic of our world. God is separate from it and sovereign over it.

This helps us understand the amazing proclamation of the seraphs: that "the whole earth *is* full of God's glory." I emphasize the present tense affirmation, that the whole earth *is now* full of God's glory, because it runs contrary to our worldly, human observation. The seraphs were exhorting Isaiah to see that God is still on the throne, ruling in glory. Isaiah had been blinded to this fact of faith. This perspective comes when we lift our eyes from the discouragement that surrounds us to see the Lord who is still bringing forth life according to His sovereign will. When Isaiah draws near to God, everything else in life takes on a new perspective. Walking by sight makes us stumble headlong, where walking by faith lets us run.

Isaiah's vision lays a strong foundation for understanding the fear of the Lord which is the beginning of wisdom (see Prov. 1:7). This healthy fear (which will be considered more thoroughly in another chapter) is rooted in a vision of the glory of God which drives all other fears away, even as a disinfectant wipes out germs.

There is a downside to a clearer vision of God, however. We may rejoice as we see the disinfectant power of glory. But a problem arises when we suddenly realize that we ourselves are germs! As Isaiah was nearly overcome by the majesty of God, he was undone by the misery of evil, his own and others, which contaminated the glory-filled earth.

Seeing Ourselves in a New Light

Isaiah's reaction reminds us of the old formula: "There's good news, and there's bad news!" The bad news is that when we view ourselves from the perspective of God's glory, we pollute the temple! "Woe to me! . . . I am ruined! For I am a man of unclean lips, and I live among a people of unclean lips, and my eyes have seen the King, the Lord Almighty" (Isa. 6:5). Isaiah is nearly overcome by the majesty of God, and then he is nearly undone by the misery of his own soul condition. "My eyes have seen the King, but now I see myself, and I am afraid." When we see God as He is, we see ourselves in a new light: a spotlight. That spotlight reveals our spots—and it can be devastating.

An honest consideration of the struggles of our society often leads us to one finger pointing out while three others point in. Dick Halverson, former Chaplain of the United States Senate, tells of a Senator speaking to a large group of parents on the subject of prayer in public schools. "How many of you believe we should have prayer in public schools?" Nearly every hand in the audience went up.

"Let me ask you a second question: How many of you prayed with your children yesterday or today?" An embarrassed silence fell on the group as only a few hands were raised.

"How can we expect the schools and our children to value prayer when we don't pray?"

That's a spotlight! "Woe to me!" we cry out. Much of the weakness of our crumbling society can be traced to our own lack of involvement. Our failure to invest in our families, our failure to care for our neighbors, our failure to mobilize our congregations, our failure to be at work in our communities, and our failure to transform the social systems have left a deficit that makes the national debt look like a parking ticket. There is a human deficit of staggering proportions.

"We are ruined!" we cry out. Once we grasp the poverty of the resources when compared to the proportions of the crisis, we are shaken to the core. Once we grasp the nature of our own liability for the problems, we may wonder how life can ever go on. The harsh beam of the spotlight exposes things we never want to see. Just when we think we cannot endure another moment, God acts.

The good news is that God's grace is greater than our guilt. Perhaps a better analogy than that of the spotlight would be that of a searchlight. Living on the coast, I saw the searchlights of the lighthouses that would scan the ocean waves, searching for those who were in trouble and guiding them to safety. The goal of God's light is not that of ridicule and condemnation that comes with exposure. God's light is for redemption from brokenness, leading us to safety through repentance and restoration. As the psalmist said,

Search me, O God, and know my heart;
    test me and know my anxious thoughts.
See if there is any offensive way in me,
    and lead me in the way everlasting.
(Ps. 139:23-24)

Fear can be like the searchlight which exposes our need and guides us toward a safe place, a healing place.

This was Isaiah's experience as a seraph which had flown with the "Holy, holy, holy Lord" now descended to the lowly, lowly, lowly man. A live coal from the holy altar touched the mouth of the unclean person, and his sin was atoned for.

A central dynamic of fear is addressed by this action. One of the most vulnerable avenues for fear's encroachment is that of our guilt and shame. When Adam and Eve heard the sound of God in the Garden, they were afraid and hid themselves because of guilt. Guilt left the door open and fear rushed in. The only way to close that door is to address the guilt at its source. That means settling the matter before the tribunal of God. Isaiah's vision shows us that God takes not only the first step, but also the final one, to free us from the bondage of guilt.

The Apostle John understood the dynamic interplay of guilt and fear. In his first letter he writes, "This is love: not that we loved God, but that He loved us and sent His Son as an atoning sacrifice for our sins" (1 John 4:10). But many of us fail to apply this verse to our lives. How many of your fears are triggered by guilt? How many of us feel that we are going to be punished for something we did long ago—that God is just waiting to trip us up. See now, the seraph flies to you! The sacrifice of Jesus ignites the burning coals of God's altar. Through faith they touch our lips. The result? We become guilt-free! This enables us to become fear-free! "There is no fear in love. But perfect love drives out fear, because fear has to do with punishment. The one who fears is not made perfect in love" (v. 18). The antidote to guilt-based fear is love. Love known and love shown.

Fear-free? Ah, maybe we are not there yet, but John promises that the way is open as we are "made perfect in love." In other words, as our experience of love matures—this is the essential meaning of perfection—our experience of guilt-based fear diminishes. As the threats of society rise, our response is not hindered by the distortion and anxiety of our own guilt. Instead we are free to act. Action is what God calls for. As we see ourselves in a new light, we see the world around us differently as well.

Taking the Offensive against That Which Offends

In these few short verses, the prophet has traversed a spiritual landscape from a desert of despair to the thin-aired heights of glory. Isaiah is a different person. He is now capable of a different response to the world he faces. He has heard the voice of the seraphs proclaiming the glory of God. His own voice has confessed the shame of his guilt. Then, another voice is heard. It is a voice of request, "Whom shall I send? And who will go for Us?"

If Isaiah had been asked this question at the start of the vision, how would he have responded? He would have been incapable of responding positively. But Isaiah's commitment now invites a commissioning to action. Without hesitation, Isaiah responds, "Here am I. Send me!" Fear has been transformed because he fixed his eyes on the horizon of faith. The nausea of soul-sickness was healed. He will no longer serve a king who will die, but One who is the author of life. He will no longer be a scribe for the pronouncements of one whose fragile throne may be toppled, but for One whose throne is from everlasting to everlasting.

Fear has been defeated, overcome by the presence of the Lord. The result is a call to go back into the world and confront the fear-inciters with the love, the truth, and the authentic fear of the Lord.

In the glorious alchemy of grace, God changes the ore of our anxiety into the gold of His service, the currency of His kingdom. Fear, then, has shaken us to our senses so that we take positive actions to transform our circumstances with the touch of Christ. These actions emerge naturally from our encounter with God. In place of the panic reflex of desperation by one overwhelmed with the fright of the immediate circumstances, the person of faith responds with the confidence of one whose hope is fixed on the horizon.

Following a Pastoral Prayer Summit conference sponsored by Northwest Renewal Ministries, a pastor named Roger Minassian, of Fresno, heard God's call to confront the rising fear in his city due to the increase of youth gangs. The Los Angeles riots of April 1992 were his wake-up call. God burned a question into his heart: "What kind of despair causes people to set fire to their own neighborhoods?" In a letter to me, Roger wrote,

> What I read from the newspapers about gang members made me ask, "How can they be so bad?" After I listened to gang members tell me their life stories of abandonment, rejection and abuse, I wondered, "How can they be so good?"
>
> I left my first meeting with gang members and began to cry. As I prayed, their pain had become mine, and I knew that somebody had to do something. Over the next few weeks, the Lord woke me up night after night with Isaiah 61:1-3, until I saw that these gang members would become "oaks of righteousness, a planting of the Lord, for the display of His splendor."[4]

Roger told me, "The only way to help these kids is to give them hope now!" Within several months, he resigned from his congregation and formed an organization he calls, "Hope Now for Youth." His strategy is to partner with churches in or near gang neighborhoods. He places a minority college student in that church with the responsibility of making contact with gang members and "wanna-be's" (young children who want to become gang members). The goal is to help the young people start a new way of life by finding a job.

The incentive for employers is that "Hope Now for Youth" equips their youth with basic skills such as courtesy, hygiene, time management, and specific work techniques so that they can sustain stable employment. The success rate for the initial placements has been very encouraging. In the first year, of the 27 youths who were placed in jobs, 25 are still employed. They have gotten 10 dropouts back in school. They have found temporary work for dozens more and are preparing nearly 100 young people for the work force. As they begin to get their lives together, the young people also discover the love of God and commit their lives to Jesus Christ, to His people, and to His service. The community at large has also been encouraged. The local television and newspapers, the mayor and city council, the business community and networks of churches are joining together through the work of "Hope Now for Youth." They see it as a practical vehicle which can channel the anxiety of fear into constructive energy for change.

This story is just one example that God does not desert a world that is caught in the icy grip of fear. First, He reveals His glory and grace to His people. Then, He sends His people to confront the sources of fear with His glorious resources. When God's people take the offensive, they can fulfill Paul's exhortation, "Do not be overcome by evil, but overcome evil with good" (Rom. 12:21).

Faith in the Known Overcomes Fear of the Unknown

Fear may never leave us in this life, but it need not rob us of joy and confidence. In Jesus Christ, we become a courageous people. Mark Twain said, "Courage is resistance to fear, mastery of fear—not absence of fear." When fear threatens and the nausea rises, we can train ourselves to look to the horizon of God's sovereign rule.

Fear is God's reveille to stir us to action. While we cannot predict the future chapters of our lives, we do know the Author. *When the fear of society's collapse threatens to overwhelm us, courageous faith awakens when we look to the Lord and receive His call to action.*

Investing in Your "R & D"
Questions for Reflection and Discussion

1. What current social trends and problems most trouble you, stirring up fear and anxiety within you?

2. What is your natural response to these troubles?

3. Has there been a situation in your experience when you have felt "the motion sickness of fear"? What emotional process did you go through?

4. When you think of Isaiah's vision of God, what aspects of the vision most impress you? Do any aspects confuse you?

5. Read Revelation 4:1-11. How is this vision similar to Isaiah's? How are they different? What effect do they have on our perspective on life?

6. Why are we told of the songs of the angels and other heavenly creatures?

7. What principles from Isaiah's experience could be most useful to you at this time?

8. What Scriptures have you found as the greatest source of courage and encouragement in times of fear?

9. What one or two fears inspire you to "take the offensive against that which offends"? What would be your first step?

Chapter Two

Looking in
Heaven's Mirror

Not all fears make us tremble. Some just make us sad. One such fear is the fear of leading an insignificant life. This fear dogs the steps of many people, especially in our competitive culture. There is the young student who chafes at the delay of studies, wanting to get out there and make a difference in the world. There is the young mother who treasures her children, but experiences strange, unwelcome feelings of being passed by as others "move up" in the world while she stays at home. There is the construction worker who can't see the value in his work when compared with his pastor. Then there are the pastors who feel like they are ineffective, struggling to keep a congregation afloat. Different people are all asking the same questions: "What difference does my life make? When will I get to do something that is really important?"

Most of us lead lives that will never make the news. Since we are tempted to equate headlines with worth, our stock seems to decline in value unless we are getting someone else's attention. This is one of the most insidious types of fear because it is so subtle and confusing. It isn't noisy like anxiety, or aggressive like anger. Its seed is self-depreciation and its fruit is apathy. When we are under the influence of this fear, we withdraw from contributing what God has given us to offer. We devalue the contributions we do make. Even worse, we hoard to ourselves the affirmations we could give others who are making significant contributions. Everyone loses when we see ourselves as insignificant.

What Mirrors Are You Using?

Who tells you who you are? When we want to know how we look, we turn to a mirror. When we want to estimate our worth, we check a variety of "mirrors." Most often, we look into the mirrors of the world. The world's mirrors, however, cannot give a true reflection of our worth. They only reflect those qualities and achievements which the world deems important. The standards of worldly significance include power, position, prestige, and possessions. The result is like looking in a "fun house mirror" whose concave and convex surfaces distort our true image. If the world's mirrors are the basis for our self-evaluation, we will experience a serious identity crisis!

The mirror we use does make a difference. Imagine a person who believes the "fun house image" that made him look squat and fat when in fact he was tall and lean. Based on that image, the person may mistakenly undertake a severely restrictive diet that weakens him, even threatening his life.

It is not a safe thing to believe the image and the applause of the world's images. Those who thrive on the sound of clapping hands may one day have to flee as those hands pick up rocks to stone them. Mansions and fame and personal bodyguards are no security from the corrosive inner forces of selfishness, sensuality, and deception, nor from the destructive outer forces of gossip and false allegations. We have only to consider the troubles faced by celebrity music stars like Michael Jackson, or by movie stars like Charlie Chaplin and Woody Allen, or by politicians like Senators Gary Hart or Robert Packwood, or by televangelists like Jim Bakker and Jimmy Swaggart, or by business leaders like Donald Trump, to realize that "significance" in the world's eyes carries tremendous liabilities. It puts incredible pressure on the fragile quality of personal character. It brings constant attention and intensive scrutiny. It conveys a system of values that actually devalue the most important things in life. Human character cannot endure much unless it is strengthened from within.

I recall hearing then-Secretary of State James A. Baker III speak at the National Prayer Breakfast in Washington, D.C. Several years before, he had a meeting with a group of diplomats in which one diplomat asked him what he felt was the most important thing he had learned since coming to Washington. Secretary of State Baker replied, "It was the discovery that *temporal power is fleeting.*" He then told about an experience he had early one morning, when serving as the White House Chief of Staff. He was riding in his limousine, bound for the White House. As his limo turned into the White House driveway, he looked down Pennsylvania Avenue and noticed a man walking alone. The man was someone many of us would have recognized—a chief of staff in a previous Administration. Yet, there he was alone—no reporters, no security, no adoring public, no trappings of power—just one solitary man alone with his thoughts.

That mental picture burned a place in Mr. Baker's consciousness, continually reminding him of the impermanence of power and position. That man had once had it *all*—but only for a time. In a reflective mood, Mr. Baker continued to address leaders from all walks of life in the United States and from around the world who had gathered for the Prayer Breakfast, "When I leave Washington, what will remain? One thing I know for *sure*—the people who wouldn't return my telephone calls *before* I went to Washington, won't return them *after I leave!*"

Secretary of State Baker looked into a mirror that morning. It was not the mirror of the world which told him he was powerful. It was a mirror of faith which reflected both the deceptions of the life and the basis for his true significance. It may have shown him something he did not want to see, but it was an image that brought him life. "Most importantly," he said, "having a position of power does *not* bring inner security and fulfillment. That comes only by developing a personal relationship with God, which for me is personified by Jesus Christ. Inner security and real fulfillment come by faith."[2]

The tragedy is that many of us neglect to look into the "mirrors of faith" in order to evaluate our worth accurately. We have believed the "fun house mirrors" of this world. They have given us false images of what is really important. They have communicated the distorted messages that we are not good enough. We have felt the sad fear of not contributing in a meaningful way. Some of us have even reached the point of wondering why we bother going on with life. Why bother? When you hear that question in your soul, it's time to shatter your old mirrors!

There Is No Such Thing As a "Justa" in God's Kingdom!

I was part of a renewal team which had assembled from a number of churches to minister in a particular congregation. Since many of us had never met, we went around the circle to introduce ourselves. The first person was a fairly well-known pastor who would be preaching. The second person was another fairly well-known musician who would provide an opening concert. The next person was a surgeon who was known for her exceptional skill and deep faith. The next person spoke quietly, "My name is Joe. I'm justa builder and layman in my church." You could almost feel something snap as he spoke. Before I knew it, I heard myself say, "Joe, there's no such thing as a 'justa!' " Joe looked puzzled, then he smiled and the group started to laugh. We all saw in a moment what many of us do consistently, even in the family of faith: we compare ourselves. We look into the mirrors of worldly accomplishment and try to see how we measure up.

In God's eyes, there's no such person as "justa laywoman," "justa layman," "justa pastor," "justa a youth worker," or "justa retired person." There are no justas! Each person has been created by God with a unique call. *God created you as you to do what only you can do!*

We have a difficult time believing this because the world has taught us to use the "utility factor" to determine the significance and value of our lives. The utility factor says that our worth is equal to our work, that our value depends on our productivity, that our significance is derived from our performance. This seems to be the intrinsic motivation behind our work ethic, though it need not necessarily be so. Joyful stewardship is a far more effective stimulus than anxious performance.

The logic of utility is heartless. It casts a cold, dark shadow over too many lives. What of the people who are physically challenged through birth defects or accidents? What of the children and older people who are not able to contribute "measurable" productivity to society? When we stop and evaluate their situations, no one with a heart would say they have no value. In fact, these people are especially valuable to us. Yet we often fail to see the logic of utility that oppresses our own lives. If we can see the irrationality of applying the utility factor to others, why can't we extend the same grace toward ourselves?

I know what it means to be haunted by the dark principality of utility. I start to itch when I sit still for too long. I feel like I need to be doing something significant, or I'm wasting oxygen. Sad! Tim Hansel's book title says it so well: *When I Relax, I Feel Guilty.* He sounds a warning to performance-driven people. He speaks with soul-rattling insight, especially as he uncovers the distorted theological rationale which drives so many of Jesus' followers. He writes,

> In our worthy attempt to avoid idleness and questionable pleasures, we begin to feel that everything must be useful. Thus, our false guilt compels us to read for profit, attend parties for contacts, exercise so we can work better, and rest in order to be more efficient. We regress to a kind of neopuritanism that says, "You have not been born into the world for pleasure." A curious and familiar psychological need to justify everything emerges, leaving no room for discovery and pure enjoyment.[3]

We feel the need to justify our existence. As if we were afraid that God would call us to account, "Well, how much oxygen did you use today? Was it worth it?" In contrast to this, Hansel suggests that we were created for pleasure. Created for pleasure? Created for pleasure. Pleasure apart from performance? Hansel asserts that God would say, "Absolutely!"

Think for a moment how much creativity God has "wasted" in this world. How many of us would have ever seen the depths of the sea apart from the wonder of marine exploration and technology? There are creatures and formations beyond imagination! God "wasted" all that? No! Why did God create giraffes? To prune tall trees? Of what utility is a giraffe? Someone in biology would want to instruct me in the principles of the food chain, but I see something more important here: God's creativity and valuing of life go far beyond utility—and so must ours. There is a delight in God's creation, including how He created us.

Savor these thoughts for a moment; roll them around in your mind. Many of us have no concept that we could be pleasing apart from our performance. The problem, you see, lies not only with the world forcing itself upon us. It lies also in our own distorted vision. In other words, not only are we using the wrong mirrors, but we cannot see clearly because of our own distorted perception. The prescription for correction comes from looking at ourselves through the lens of God's Word.

We Are Handcrafted Treasures

One of the most affirming principles of Scripture is that each of us is handcrafted by God. In Psalm 139:13-16 we read,

> For You created my inmost being;
>   You knit me together in my mother's womb.
> I praise You because I am fearfully and wonderfully made;
>   Your works are wonderful,
> I know that full well.
> My frame was not hidden from You
>   when I was made in the secret place.
> When I was woven together in the
>   depths of the earth,
>   Your eyes saw my unformed body.

The intimacy and tenderness of these words is beyond comprehension. They present us with images of God "knitting us together," molding us, shaping us, forming us with the touch of love and care and gentleness. We are fearfully and wonderfully made. Do you "know that full well"? The psalmist does. David knows that none of us is mass-produced! We are each the unique work of the Master Artist. There is no one like you in the world! Never has been! Never will be! No one has your mix of personality characteristics, talents, skills, interests, family history, personal experiences, and present-day circumstances. No one! These facts alone can help us understand that there is no place for comparison with others. We cannot look into anybody else's mirror.

The love expressed in Psalm 139 is reserved not only for David, but for all God calls His own. God has no favorite children. He cherishes each of us, having shaped us from the moment of our conception. David even goes so far as to say, "All the days ordained for me were written in Your book, before one of them came to be" (v. 16). This verse contains truth so simple that a child can understand it, and truth so complex that a lifetime of meditation will never exhaust it. The simple truth is that God cares about everything that happens to you every day. All your days and nights are so important that God has them recorded in His heavenly journals. The complex truth is that God works in a way that guides our lives according to His will while at the same time honoring our personal integrity and responsibility. These are the deep waters of theology which teem with life for those who will brave them. But we do not have to plunge into their depths to receive the main point: each of us matters to God, from our first temporal breath to our last. Before we can do anything to earn God's love, we already have it! Again, we must celebrate and affirm this great truth: *God created you as you to do what only you can do!*

My conversations with others and my own self-talk have taught me that we have a difficult time believing these things. Too many of us suffer from what I call "The Eeyore Syndrome." Eeyore is the donkey in the "Winnie the Pooh" series of books by A.A. Milne. He is a lovable but dour character who slouches through life, expecting to be neglected, abused, and unappreciated. His basic attitude comes through when he says, "Go ahead, step on me ... break my back. ... It's OK. Don't worry about me."

God did not create anyone to be an "Eeyore." God created us to be heroes! Heroes of everyday faithfulness. Paul's words in Ephesians 1 and 2 proclaim this vigorously. "For God chose us in Christ before the creation of the world. . . . In love He predestined us to be adopted as His sons (and daughters!) through Jesus Christ. . . . For we are God's workmanship, created in Christ Jesus to do good works, which God prepared in advance for us to do" (see 1:4-5 and 2:10). Arguments about predestination aside, these verses boldly affirm that from eternity, every single person God calls is special. God measures our significance from the starting point of love and by our response of faith and faithfulness.

Our value is intrinsic, not extrinsic. In other words, we are valuable and significant from the very start of life. We do not accumulate value over time, based on check stubs, press clippings, offices held, or plaques on the wall. These are better understood as expressions of the value we have always possessed.

Looking in the Mirror of Love

When we understand with our hearts, not just our minds, that we are handcrafted treasures, we begin to understand God's standards of significance. We were not created to earn value, but with value. We are not His workmanship to be set on the shelf to be admired. We were created for "good works which God prepared in advance for us to do" (Eph. 2:10). What are those good works?

The response is found in Jesus' words to the one who asked,

"Teacher, which is the greatest commandment in the Law?" Jesus replied: " 'Love the Lord your God with all your heart and with all your soul and with all your mind.' This is the first and greatest commandment. And the second is like it: 'Love your neighbor as yourself.' All the Law and the Prophets hang on these two commandments" (Matt. 22:36-39).

Our significance is measured by love. Apart from love, all our accomplishments are nothing. With love, every accomplishment is something special.

As we have received love, we reflect love. We become heaven's mirrors. People need to be able to look into us and see the reflection of their worth to God. The only way we can reflect their worth is if we have seen our worth reflected from God.

When we view life from God's perspective, we develop new criteria for valuing what is important. We value human creativity and achievement in all areas which honor God. We also know, however, the value of the person apart from anything she can do or contribute. This perspective is essential if we are to value, for example, infant children and those who are physically or mentally limited by illness or age. The point is not what they can or cannot do, but the fact that they are created in the image of God. This is the foundation of all value.

I do not pretend to be an economist, but this I know: the value of United States currency is no longer based on the "objective" gold standard (as objective as any such standard can be), but on a much more politically dependent standard set by the Federal Reserve Board. The Federal Reserve Board can regulate the value of the dollar, including devaluing it, because the dollar is no longer backed by a material resource, but by government policy.

Such a system may be wise for economics, but it is devastating when applied to human beings. Human worth cannot be regulated by any human system. Such attempts lead to the horrors of Hitler's Nazism. We live by the "God standard," the gold standard of life. Human lives are valued on the standards established by the Creator. Even though we have degraded ourselves through disobedience to the Creator, He has not devalued us. In fact, He has confirmed our supreme value by sending His own Son to be one of us and buy us back.

The starting place for each of us to assess our net worth is with the valuation attributed to us by the God who made us. What significance do we attach to being "fearfully and wonderfully made"? What do the scales read when we step on them with the robe of royal adoption that is ours in Christ? What do others around us think when the Lord of life calls us over, puts His arms around us and says, "Call Me Dad"?

When you know you are loved, you are free to make a difference, a loving difference, in others' lives.

Leading a Value-added Life

One of the most practical ways that we can make a significant contribution immediately is to add positive value to everything we do. This concept is inspired by Richard Bolles in his best-selling book, *What Color Is Your Parachute?* At the core of his concept of developing a life mission statement is the premise that we are in this world to make it a better place. How? Not by end results alone, but by the moment-by-moment decisions we make that add more love to the world, or less; more honesty, or less; more or less forgiveness, more or less gratitude. Now, picture this scene: you're traveling the freeway in heavy traffic and come to a part under construction. The left lanes need to merge to the right. You see it is clear driving in the left lane for a short way ahead, but you merge over patiently. Then someone zooms past you on the left to avoid the slowed traffic. You have been patient. You merged courteously and have been creeping along very slowly. Now, you reach the spot where the "zoomer" is trying to merge, but no one will let him. You have a choice: I call it the choice between "Serves 'em right!" or "How can I serve 'em right?" (I realize that proper English dictates that the correct word is 'rightly'—but it doesn't have the same punch!) Will you add more anger or less on the highways? The choice makes our life significant. The smallest decision can make the biggest difference.

The same principle applies when we are dealing with a difficult person. Jesuit priest and communications professor John Powell says, "The fully human person is an Actor, not a Reactor." By that he does not mean "actor" in the sense of one who plays a part, but in the sense of one who is proactive and takes action independent of the circumstances. He tells the story of Sydney Harris, the syndicated columnist, who was accompanying his friend to a newsstand. The friend greeted the newsstand attendant courteously, but was met with gruff, discourteous service. Accepting the newspaper which was rudely shoved to him, Harris' friend smiled politely and

worm
or serpent

wished the attendant a nice weekend.

As the two friends walked down the street, Harris asked: "Does he always treat you so rudely?"

"Oh, yes, unfortunately."

"And are you always so polite and friendly to him?"

"Yes, I am."

"Why?"

"Because I don't want him to decide how I'm going to act."[4]

Seeing ourselves in God's mirror first sets us free to see every one and every situation differently. As we consider each situation, we ask ourselves: do I want to add more anger now, or less? More calmness or less? More integrity or less? Our decisions in these brief moments can have lasting significance.

The Little Things Make the Big Difference in Life

In love, the little things we do have the most significance for others. The details say we care. On one of our youth mission trips to Mexico, one of the student leaders, Stephanie, took it upon herself to write a personal note to each of the students and advisers during the seven days. She would "target" six or seven people a day, taking time to observe what they were doing. Then she wrote a few sentences expressing appreciation for something specific she saw. The trip was transformed. She held up heaven's mirror to those on the team. The affect was consistent: when you look in heaven's mirror, you become heaven's mirror. By the third day, notes and words of affirmation were flowing freely among the team members because Stephanie showed the team what joy it brought. She was significant because she let others know how significant they were.

Looking in the Mirror of Our Gifts

In addition to looking into the mirror of love, God longs for us to experience the significance which flows from the stewardship of our gifts. This stewardship may not gain the world's attention, but it makes heaven's headlines.

Satisfaction begins with developing a biblical perspective on our activities. Somewhere I heard the story of two men at work in a stone quarry. When one was asked what he was doing, he replied, "I'm getting the rock out of this pit." The other responded, "I'm building a cathedral!" Both doing the same task; each viewing it differently. Many of us are like the first man, seeing only the unglamorous task of the moment. But the Lord calls us to lift our eyes. Imagine the surprise of those who heard the words of the Lord, "I tell you the truth, whatever you did for one of the least of these brothers of Mine, you did for Me" (Matt. 25:40).

Our "significance quotient" is woven into the desires of our hearts. As we exercise the gifts God has given us and pursue the interests we most deeply enjoy, it is most likely that we will be pleasing to God. We will also experience a wholesome satisfaction that we are doing the right thing. In the movie *Chariots of Fire*, Eric Liddell was chastised by his sister for his interest in running. She felt he should be serving as a missionary. "All I know," he told his sister, "is that when I run, I feel His pleasure." Liddell went on to run in the Olympic Games and presented a powerful testimony to his faith not only in his own generation, but also to those who have followed.

When we share what we have with Jesus, He makes our lives significant. One of my favorite illustrations of this is the feeding of the 5,000. This story tells us of an overwhelming need and of people who could have felt that their lives were too insignificant and inadequate for that need. John vividly portrays a situation in which an unknown person, who shared what little he had, made possible an extraordinary expression of God's promise and power.

Massive crowds were following Jesus. They were feasting on the wonder of His teaching and His miracles. In fact, they were so caught up with Jesus that they failed to plan for eating. According to John's Gospel, Jesus recognized the need and asked Philip, "Where shall we buy bread for these people to eat?" (John 6:5)

Philip responded realistically, "Eight months wages' would not buy enough bread for each one to have a bite!" Practically speaking, there are many times in life when we are tempted to be overwhelmed by circumstances. We feel insignificant because we see our inadequacy. This was the disciples' reaction.

Then, Andrew spoke up. As a person of some foresight, he may have been thinking about this problem for some time, exploring all options. "Here is a boy with five small barley loaves and two small fish, but how far will they go among so many?"

Andrew saw some resources, but they seemed so inadequate, so insignificant in the face of such great need.

But for Jesus, it was enough. How much does Jesus need to make a difference?

When you look in heaven's mirror, you see a loving Lord looking over your shoulder, pointing to what you are holding, and inviting you to use it.

What do you have in your hands? How is the Lord inviting you to share it with Jesus and with the hungry world? The boy Andrew spotted didn't have to start a bakery, or develop a slick marketing system, or establish a dynasty through the "Barley Loaf Brotherhood," or "Faithful Fish Society"! He simply made what he had available to meet the needs of that moment. He was not under the illusion that he had to provide for everybody. Instead, he decided he would at least provide for somebody. And God took care of the rest.

It's interesting to see that this miracle is the only one besides the Resurrection which is recorded in all four Gospels. One reason could well be its message of promise for us as we face all manner of intimidating demands. "Make yourself available," says the Lord, "and I will use you. Then I will make the headlines in your life, and you will make the headlines in heaven."

When we are confronted by the fear that all our efforts have added up to nothing, that in the grand scheme of things, we are like dust on the scales, it's time to look in heaven's mirror. See the reflection of a royal child, purchased with a King's ransom, clothed in the robe of spotless purity. Then say to yourself, "God created me as me to do what only I can do." In the final analysis, the measure of our significance will not be the volume of our achievements, but the depth, the height, and the breadth of His from-the-beginning love.

INVESTING IN YOUR "R & D"
QUESTIONS FOR REFLECTION AND DISCUSSION

1. In what ways have you felt insignificant? Think of people, classroom experiences, work situations, community activities, and church groups that have influenced your feelings.

most of my life - The Lord brought Significance to me

2. What is your image of a "significant" life? What are the "fun house mirrors" you are most tempted to look into? Where did that image come from?

what I do for Jesus + others around me

3. If someone younger asked you, "What is the most important thing in life?" what would you say? How does that match with your image of significance?

Jesus - pleasing Him

4. Secretary of State James Baker said that the most important lesson he learned was that temporal power is fleeting. What examples of this have you seen? How have you experienced this in your own life? *Fame is fleeting.*
Do things in light of eternity

5. Read Psalm 139.

   sin still loves us

   a. Why does the psalmist begin with the fact that "God has searched" him and "known" him? What has God's search revealed? How has it affected God's love toward him?

   b. What is the attitude described in verses 5-12? What does this tell us about God's love?

   humble

   c. Verses 13-16 affirm the value of our lives from the very beginning. How do you feel saying to yourself, "I am fearfully and wonderfully made"?

   His people need Him to live the way they sh—

   d. In this psalm, verses 19-22 show us that David was being threatened by enemies who were out to get him. How do the thoughts of the previous verses help him face these threats? What threats do you face (though maybe you would not describe them with such strong language) that make you question your significance and security? *betrayal.*

   e. How is the invitation for God to search the heart in verses 22-24 different from the first search described in verse 1?

   f. How is this psalm a mirror of heaven for you?

6. What "little things" has someone done for you that have let you know you are loved? *a hug, a helping hand, a prayer, acceptance through trials*

7. Jesus accepted five small loaves and two fish from a boy, and used them to create a meal for 5,000. What could you offer up to God that could be used to make a big difference in someone else's life? Make a plan and go for it!
prayer

8. A main theme of this chapter is the principle that "God created you as you to do what only you can do." What are some of the special qualities of your life, your personality, your experiences, and life situation that give you some clues as to how God would like to use you?

teacher -
worshipper -
bring healing & comfort to others

Chapter Three

Soaring on Wings of Encouragement

There are three questions we ask whenever we interact with others: Will you like me? Will you accept me? Will you receive my gifts? All of these are questions concerning acceptance and rejection. The response we receive will have a dramatic impact on our relationships.

When I was in elementary school, I played with two friends I will call Rick and Bill. One day, Rick pulled me aside and said, "Let's ditch Bill." I thought it sounded like fun, so we lost him on a bike ride and avoided him after school for two days. When we got back together with Bill, he was angry and hurt. That soon seemed to be forgotten, and we played together for a week or so. One day, we went into a convenience store to get some candy. When I paid and went back outside, Rick and Bill were nowhere to be found! I'd been ditched. Now that was a different story, and I didn't think it was very funny. I can vividly remember the hot tears I kept wiping from my eyes as I rode home. I could never quite trust those two again. But Bill and I had both learned a lesson from Rick. That's right—we ditched him!

The fear of rejection shakes us to the core. Whether it's in grade school, graduate school, or the school of hard knocks, nobody likes to be ditched. We were made for community, for friendship, for acceptance, and belonging. When the Lord said, "It is not good for the man to be alone" (Gen. 2:18), He was not merely referring to a marriage companion, but to our communal nature. We want to be liked, to be valued, to belong to a group. But many factors seem to work against the human connection. One evidence of this is the acknowledgment by many that they have few people they really trust as friends.

The fear of rejection affects people in a variety of ways. Some overfunction in an effort to be liked or appreciated. They think that their activity will insure their acceptance. Others function in a more defensive way, carefully guarding themselves against overexposure lest someone take advantage of them. Their premise is that you cannot be rejected if you have not asked to be accepted. Whether doting or defensive, such reactions generate an anxious undercurrent of fear, making relationships more of a burden than a blessing.

Exploring the Roots of Rejection

The fear of rejection arises from a number of sources, but the tap root is our legitimate need to be connected with and valued by others. If we are honest, many would admit that we feel the need for the approval of others above the need for God's approval. We may try to excuse this as the result of confidence that "things are already settled" with God. More likely, however, is the fact that we crave the admiration, affection, and positive attention of our peers. This unhealthy craving creates an orientation of depending on others for what we can only find in the Lord. We will consider this more fully in a moment, but first, let's explore several different levels of rejection.

There are at least three different levels of rejection:

First is the fear of rejection we face when entering or seeking to be included in a new group. We experience "introduction anxiety" when we meet new people and wonder if they will accept us and value us as people. The "dance" begins in which we search for those reference points that give us clues as to "where this person is coming from," to use the vernacular. Topics such as schools attended, career interests, favorite books, and political opinions are used as we try to map the geography of the relationship. A person with a personality preference for extroversion finds this process fascinating and is carefully tuned to the response of the other. An introverted person usually finds this very difficult, but may be freer from undue concern about the other person's reaction because her values are more inner-directed than those of the extrovert. My point is not to develop a psychology of personality types and rejection, but to highlight the fact that we each, different as we are, confront the dynamics of "introduction anxiety."

A second level of rejection arises from conflicting values. When our ideas and values clash with others, we are often faced with the choice of either compromising or being cut off from the group. A teenager may be pressured to either join in or leave at a party where everybody else is drinking alcohol. A business-person who refuses to falsify warranty information may face ostracism from those who could most help her career. A lay leader in a congregation may feel strongly that a certain doctrine or practice should no longer be ignored, only to find himself ignored by those who disagree. The satisfaction of being true to conscience is tainted by the relational cost of taking a heartfelt stand.

A third level of rejection is that of persecution for the cause of Christ. We are told by Jesus to anticipate persecution. "If the world hates you, keep in mind that it hated Me first. . . . Remember the words I spoke to you: 'No servant is greater than his master.' If they persecuted Me, they will persecute you also" (John 15:18, 20). Though this may be the most dramatic and costly rejection to bear in a physical and material sense, it can be made more bearable by the knowledge that we are standing in a noble company of the faithful across the centuries who have testified to their faith on the witness stands of public humiliation and worse.

Other types of rejection could be enumerated, but these three levels give us a general overview of the relational land-scape we want to navigate. How do you go forward?

On the Journey into Acceptance

The force-field of this fear is broken by the magnetic attrac-tion of the God who created us. We are called to live in the knowledge that we by faith in Jesus Christ are accepted: accepted by God as daughters and sons, called to accept one another in the love of God. This wonderful truth is at the heart of the biblical doctrine of justification. Richard Lovelace defines the theological term justification in these simplest terms: "You are accepted." We are not accepted on the basis of our parentage, our performance, or our theological pedigree. God's grace in Jesus Christ is much, much greater than anything we could ever provide for ourselves. Lovelace writes,

> Many have a theoretical commitment to this doctrine, but in their day-to-day existence they rely on their sanctification for justification. . . . Few know enough to start each day with a thoroughgoing stand upon Luther's platform: *you are accepted,* looking outward in faith and claiming the wholly alien righteousness of Christ as the only ground for acceptance, relaxing in that quality of trust which will produce increasing sanctification as faith is active in love and gratitude.[1]

God has rejected the rejection of sin through Jesus Christ! We are now accepted in Him. What greater acceptance could there be?

Have you ever noticed that the acceptance of one person can make you feel "at home" no matter where you are? As I sit waiting in airports, I am fascinated to observe the change in people's faces as they are waiting for arriving planes. Their faces may be blank or even have a sour expression. Then, their friend or loved one arrives and their faces light up! They are often unabashed at showing affection, even among a crowd of strangers. Why? Because they have been caught up in the power of acceptance.

God's acceptance enables us to keep human relationships, and especially the threat of rejection, in perspective. The psalmist knew this as he wrote,

> The Lord is my light and my salvation —
>   whom shall I fear?
> The Lord is the stronghold of my life —
>   of whom shall I be afraid?
>
> (Ps. 27:1)

The Apostle Paul also spoke to this point in Colossians 3:23-24. These words which speak primarily of our vocation also address our general orientation toward life and relationships. "Whatever you do, work at it with all your heart, as working for the Lord, not for men, since you know that you will receive an inheritance from the Lord as a reward. It is the Lord Christ you are serving." Fear makes us slaves of others. When we live in the confidence of God's approval, we have freedom to serve others apart from their reaction to us. In fact, our experience of God's approval enables us to cultivate a climate of acceptance and affirmation for others, who are often trapped in the fear of rejection.

We soar above the fear of rejection on the wings of the Lord's encouragement for us and our encouragement for others. Scripture contains some moving stories of encouragement, such as that of Ruth and Naomi and that of David and Jonathan. For me, however, the most powerful story is that of Joseph, a Levite from Cyprus. Does his name ring a bell with you? We first read about him in Acts 4. Joseph was one of the early believers who was deeply moved by the message of Jesus Christ. As a Levite, he was familiar with the Jewish ritual and the meaning of the sacrifice. We can only imagine what it must have meant to him when he heard that Jesus was the Messiah, the fulfillment of all that was represented by the temple sacrifices and services.

Joseph came to the special attention of the apostles because of his generosity and its impact on the community of believers. They gave Joseph an affectionate nickname: Barnabas, or "son of encouragement" (Acts 4:36). Barnabas did more than any person recorded in Scripture to overcome the practical tensions and threats of rejection that arise within the fellowship. The first evidence of the worthiness of his nickname comes from Acts 4 where we see him encourage those who are in need.

Encouraging Those in Need

Rejection can be experienced at a physical level, when we feel excluded due to practical needs. This was a problem in the

Jerusalem church. There are downsides to growth that the experts don't often highlight. As the early church grew dramatically, they faced the practical stresses of multiplied needs. Masses of people were coming to faith, especially the poor. Think of the apostles' frustration at not being able to provide for the widows, the orphans, and others in dire straits. But the Lord not only set people free from bondage to sin, He also liberated them from greed and selfishness. "There were no needy persons among them. For from time to time those who owned lands or houses sold them, brought the money from the sales and put it at the apostles' feet, and it was distributed to anyone as he had need" (Acts 4:34-35).

Barnabas was one of those who sold his real estate in order to invest in the community of faith. He sold his land and gave the proceeds—no strings attached—to the apostles. The love of Jesus had given him a new definition of "family," and a new purpose for the use of his resources. Barnabas knew the truth of Jesus' teaching: "It is more blessed to give than to receive" (20:35). It is more blessed because you double the joy through both providing and encouraging. His love generated joy and generosity among the believers. He knew the power of money as a servant of others. Stingy lives are discouraging, but generosity is a profound encourager.

My personal sense is that Barnabas' response was not determined by the worthiness of the people's need to receive, but by what he had received in Christ. I am reminded of the story that is told of a beggar who sat by the roadside and asked for alms from Alexander the Great of Greece as he passed by. The man was poor and wretched and had no claim upon the ruler. Nevertheless, the emperor threw him several gold coins. A servant accompanying Alexander was astonished at his generosity and commented, "Sir, copper coins would adequately meet a beggar's need. Why give him gold?" Alexander responded in royal fashion, "Copper coins would suit the beggar's need, but gold coins suit Alexander's giving."[2]

We do not share the egocentricity of Alexander, but he highlights an important principle we might paraphrase this way: "Our best gift suits our Savior's gift to us." Our gifts of acceptance and support are God-inspired, not situation-dependent. This radically alters our motivation. We do not allow material considerations to influence our acceptance of others or our sense of self-worth.

But this is only our first glimpse of Barnabas. His ministry broadens until we meet him again in Acts 9.

Welcoming Those Who Are Outsiders

The fear of rejection is highest when we are trying to enter a new group. We are like lobsters who've shed the protective shell of belonging to one group, standing alone and vulnerable.

A Jew named Saul was dedicated to one cause: the extermination of the upstart challengers who claimed that the trouble-maker Jesus, who had just been crucified, was resurrected from the dead. Saul was dead-set, literally, against all who were spreading this heresy. He also shared the practical concern that this movement was endangering the Jews by antagonizing the Romans. He stood approvingly when Stephen, a spokesman for the followers of Jesus, was stoned to death. Saul's determination was firmly set by the stoning. His righteous passion was awakened, leading him to seek letters of permission to travel to outlying cities and quench the spreading flame of heresy.

On the way to tackle Jesus' followers in Damascus, the Lord threw a body block on Saul. As Saul looked up from the ground, he could see nothing, but he heard the voice of the Lord. For three days he lost his appetite both for food and for vengeance on the followers of Jesus. But a new hunger was awakening within him.

While Saul was examining everything he had ever believed, the Lord came to one of Jesus' followers in Damascus, Ananias, and called him to go to Saul. That's sort of like inviting a rabbit to come to a barbecue at a fox's lair! But Ananias obeyed the Lord. He went to the man who had been "breathing threats and murder against the disciples of the Lord." There he saw Saul, the former firebrand, now groping in darkness, longing for the light. When Ananias laid hands on him, scales fell from Saul's eyes and his soul. He was baptized and proclaimed that Jesus Christ is the Son of God. The passion for God which had turned him against Christ was now channeled into a passion for Christ. As he preached to the Jews, he himself became the target of a murder plot. He barely escaped Damascus with his life and fled to Jerusalem.

Not everyone in Jerusalem was as trusting as Ananias and the Damascus believers had been. "When he [Saul] came to Jerusalem, he tried to join the disciples, but they were all afraid of him, not believing he really was a disciple" (Acts 9:27). Jesus' followers walked daily by the pile of stones which marked the grave of Stephen. They believed Saul would stop at nothing to exterminate them. Saul's "conversion" was probably just a devious ploy to get into their midst and destroy them all.

Saul was like a man without a country. He was rejected by the Jews and shunned by the believers. Now what? Enter Barnabas. "But Barnabas took him and brought him to the apostles, told them how Saul on his journey had seen the Lord and that the Lord had spoken to him, and how in Damascus he had preached fearlessly in the name of Jesus" (v. 27). Barnabas opened the door to Saul's acceptance. He took the risk of getting to know Saul before judging and rejecting him.

Barnabas was not a prisoner of the snap judgments of others. The foolishness of such judgments is well illustrated by a story the late Bishop Potter of New York used to tell on himself.

He was sailing for Europe on a transatlantic liner. When he went on board, he found he would be sharing a cabin with another. After going to see his accommodations, he came up to the purser's desk in order to leave his gold watch and other valuables in the ship's safe. He explained that this was not his customary practice, but that he had been to his cabin and had met the man who was to occupy the other berth. Judging from his appearance, the bishop was afraid that he might not be a trustworthy person.

The purser accepted the responsibility of caring for the valuables, and remarked; "It's all right, Bishop. I'll be very glad to take care of them for you. The other man, your cabin mate, has been up here and left his for the same reason."[3]

Barnabas did not pass judgment based on appearances. I can imagine Barnabas taking Saul to a leisurely lunch. As the appetizers were served, Barnabas began, "So Saul, sounds like you have an incredible story. Tell me all about it." With compassion and discernment, Barnabas listened not only to Saul's words, but to his heart. His worst fears were allayed and, to his great joy and delight, he saw the mighty hand of God at work in another resurrection. Barnabas put skin on the grace of God. He demonstrated love in action, setting Saul free from a dark past. His encouragement enabled Saul to start all over again in the place of his biggest mistake, near the rock pile of Stephen.

Following their time together, Barnabas took Saul to a meeting with the Jerusalem disciples. He told Saul's story for him, as an advocate. The group listened and trusted Barnabas' judgment. Why? Because I think some of them had found the grace of God coming to them through Barnabas. He had listened to them in their pain and discouragement. He had backed them up. Barnabas took a chance on people.

If our congregations are to be welcoming places, it must begin with us. One day two women contacted me and said they wanted to speak to me about what the Lord had revealed to them in prayer. They had been praying for our fellowship and were eager to discuss it with me. When we met, Joanna said, "When we initially started to pray we were filled with a critical attitude and a concern with how the church wasn't meeting our needs. We are both relatively new to this congregation, but have not felt included. As we continued in prayer, the Lord showed us that we were part of the problem, and that He didn't want to change the church until He began to change us." They then asked for my support and encouragement for an initiative: "If we've felt this way, we're probably not alone. We'd like to set up a series of congregation-wide dinners in homes." The idea took off. We called them "Suppers for Seven," so we were always certain to include at least one single person. I have since heard of similar ideas, but we were undertaking a new adventure, trying an idea that was new to us in order to cultivate a welcoming climate.

It isn't enough, however, to welcome others. People feel most valued when they can contribute. Barnabas again models this principle for us.

Encouraging Others to Take Responsibility

It's easy to be intimidated by experts. When we compare ourselves to others, we often feel insignificant and inadequate. We hesitate to take a chance and offer our ideas or talents on the public stage. An encourager can make all the difference at a time like this.

As the good news of Jesus Christ spread, people responded in great numbers. In Antioch, the huge response moved the church in Jerusalem to send someone who could establish the new believers both in the understanding of the faith and the love of community. Enter Barnabas. He could get believers fired up without scorching them with demands of legalism or the disillusionment of unrealistic expectations. But Barnabas saw another need: the need to involve others in the ministry. He knew that the spread of the Gospel depended on the cultivation of leaders. So Barnabas went to Tarsus and sought out his old friend, Saul. For a year, Barnabas and Saul nurtured the new community of faith in Antioch.

Barnabas saw Antioch as a laboratory of faith in which he could shepherd Saul as together they discipled a group of new believers from the start. This too is part of the ministry of encouragement. An encourager listens not only to a person's story, but to that person's heart-desires, gifts, and sense of call from God. Then, she looks for opportunities for the person to use them. The fear of rejection is dealt with by carefully planning for the natural introduction of the person to new responsibilities.

Wise encouragement means standing alongside a person as he steps out in the risk of service. Too often we put people in situations of pressure. Maxie Dunnam tells the humorous story about a rich Texas rancher who threw a party for all his friends.

For the entertainment at the party, he filled his Olympic-size swimming pool with sharks. In the course of the evening, he invited the guests to stand around the pool while he announced that if any young man would jump in and swim across the pool, he would give him one of three things: "You may have my ranch, a million dollars, or the hand of my daughter in marriage," he said. A commotion at the other end of the pool claimed everyone's attention. One man had jumped in and frantically swam across the pool, fighting off the sharks in the churning, boiling water. Miraculously he made it to the other side safely. The rancher was dumbfounded. "I didn't think any one would take me up on that offer, but I'm a man of my word. What do you want? You can have one of three choices—my ranch, a million dollars, or you can have my daughter's hand in marriage." The exhausted man dragged himself from the water. "I don't want any of those things," he gasped. Shocked even more, the rancher said, "All right, you name it and I'll get it for you." The man said, "I want the guy that shoved me into the pool!"[4]

When we want to encourage others to take a chance, let's be sure there are no sharks in the pool, or at least that they aren't pushed in without repellant!

The ministry of encouragement enables confidence to grow through experience. We also find that community develops through sharing a task together. Barnabas and Saul worked so well together that they were designated as a team (Acts 13:2). They set out on an expedition we now call the "first missionary journey." During this journey, Saul emerges with a more prominent role in ministry. In Acts 13:9 we learn that Saul is beginning to go by a new name, Paul. The Hebrew name Saul means "asked of God." The name Paul is of non-Jewish background and means "little." Many reasons are offered for the name change (such as the name being an indication that they are now entering the Gentile phase of ministry), but my personal view is that Paul was truly coming "into his own" under the tutelage of Barnabas. His new name, like that of Simon

Peter, emphasized his new identity in Christ.

Paul takes the lead in this time of ministry. He rebukes Elymas the sorcerer, revealing his spiritual wisdom, courage, and authority. Then, as many have noted, Luke, the author of Acts, changes the typical designation of "Barnabas and Saul" to "Paul and Barnabas" (v. 43), to indicate Paul's significant leadership.

Barnabas has opened the door to Paul's highest calling in Christ. He refused to erect barriers of self-interest or competition which would block Paul's progress. Instead of competing with Paul, he celebrated him. He wanted the best for Paul and for God's people, so he lovingly pushed Paul ahead. An encourager does everything in his power to help another succeed. He has learned to overcome the fear of being upstaged and the fear that he will be rejected if someone else is accepted.

Perhaps the most profound witness of Barnabas, the son of encouragement, is that of Acts 15. Here we see the real threat of rejection handled in a manner that shows how even the best of us is vulnerable to rejecting others when they most need us.

Accepting People Who Have Failed

Paul wanted to revisit the churches of their first missionary journey. Barnabas was eager to join him and wanted to take his cousin, John Mark, along. John Mark had begun the first missionary journey, but for reasons which are not explained, he had left Paul and Barnabas and returned to Jerusalem (Acts 13:13). Paul had been and was still angry with John Mark for deserting them. He refused to take John Mark with them on this trip. Instead, Paul chose Silas to travel with him.

Barnabas remained true to his name. He was put in the predicament of choosing between Paul and John Mark. I can almost read his thoughts: *Who needs me more? Paul or John Mark? Paul? We love each other, and God has blessed our ministry together. If I don't go with him, I know we will get back together. He's stubborn, but he'll get over it . . .*

John Mark? Barnabas continues to muse. *He deserted us; yes, he failed to follow through—but now he's back! It was not easy for him to face Paul and admit his mistake. I know he's changed.*

He can do it, I know he can. John Mark needs to see that God can still use him.

Turning from his thoughts, Barnabas looks at Paul, then at John Mark. Barnabas quietly walks over and gives Paul a hug. No words are exchanged. Then he steps over to John Mark. "Let's go, son."

Barnabas opened a door out of failure for John Mark, just as he had done for Saul years before. He knew how to stop rejection and become a bridge of hope to a new future.

In this instance, Paul was vulnerable to his experience of being disappointed by one he had trusted and relied on. He was sick with the poison of bitterness. He forgot that bitterness is a poison of our own making. The hurt we receive is but one small ingredient. But mix in a measure of pride, a dash of vengeance, a pinch of self-pity, and an ounce of fear and you have concocted a malicious mixture which is certain to make you miserable.

An encourager, however, holds the antidote to bitterness. No matter how deep the pain, the one who longs for healing knows that acceptance, not rejection, is the only road back to wholeness. Charles Bracelen Flood describes a vivid experience of this in the life of Robert E. Lee, former Confederate General, following the Civil War between the States.

> After a tremendous struggle of conscience, Robert E. Lee reached the hard decision that his first loyalty was to Virginia, and took up arms in the Civil War. As General, he gave his all for the Confederate cause. But when the war was over, he worked diligently for reconciliation.
>
> Still, conciliation was his creed. Lee knew that the war was over and that everything depended on a new attitude for a new day. He was taken to call on a lady who lived north of Lexington, and she promptly showed him the remains of a tree in her yard. All its limbs had been shot off by Federal artillery fire during Hunter's raid, and its trunk was torn by cannonballs. The woman looked at him expectantly as she showed him this memento of what she and her property had

endured. Here was a man who would sympathize.

Lee finally spoke. "Cut it down, my dear madam, and forget it."[5]

Barnabas' ministry was based on the same principle. He was the type who uprooted the saplings of resentment and anger before they had time to become trees of bitterness.

People used to say that behind every great man was a great woman urging him on. We have become much more sensitive to such gender stereotypes, but it does articulate a principle we could state in more general terms: Behind every person who accomplishes meaningful things, there must be at least one person who didn't give up on that person when he was ready to give up on himself. There must have been at least one person who took a chance on her when no one else would.

Barnabas never gave up on John Mark. Approximately twelve year later, Paul wrote, "My fellow prisoner Aristarchus sends you his greetings, as does Mark, the cousin of Barnabas. (You have received instructions about him; if he comes to you, welcome him.) Jesus, who is called Justus, also sends greetings. These are the only Jews among my fellow workers for the kingdom of God, and they have been a comfort to me" (Col. 4:10-11). John Mark made it—because of Barnabas.

Soaring on the Wings of Encouragement

The early church and the church of today soar on the wings of encouragement provided by Barnabas. He encouraged Saul/Paul by showing grace and acceptance when others were still suspicious over his past. He opened the door of opportunity to Paul, calling forth the fullest expression of his gifts. If there had been no Barnabas, how would the Gospel seed have been scattered to Asia and beyond? Would we have the letters, such as Romans and Philippians, which have formed the foundation of Christian doctrine and devotion for nearly 2,000 years? What if there had been no Barnabas for Paul?

But Barnabas gave us even more. He encouraged John Mark when even Paul wouldn't. Mark went on to become a significant servant of Jesus Christ. Scholarly studies indicate that it is likely that Mark associated closely with the Apostle Peter and recorded Peter's story in an account we now call the Gospel according to Mark! Mark has been used to open the eyes of literally millions! What if there had been no Barnabas for Mark?

The question naturally arises: who needs your encouragement? Is there a Saul in your life or in your fellowship, who needs acceptance and a new chance? Is there a Mark who has failed and needs an opportunity to begin again? When you know that acceptance of the Living Lord, you are free to experiment with the greatest power in the universe: the power of love's acceptance and affirmation. Take a chance on somebody. Give them wings and watch them soar.

INVESTING IN YOUR "R & D"
QUESTIONS FOR REFLECTION AND DISCUSSION

1. In which of the three levels of rejection do you find yourself most vulnerable? Why?
   a. "Introduction anxiety"—the fear of rejection we face when entering or seeking to be included in a new group.
   b. "The Values-clash"—when our ideas and values clash with others.
   c. Rejection and persecution for your faith.

2. Which characteristic or situation of Barnabas' encouragement strikes you as most important? Why? *When Paul was rejected by all. He accepted him.*

3. Who has been a Barnabas to you? When? Have you ever *Adele* taken time to thank them (and God!) for what they did? *Jan Peg, Ruth + Theo, Linda Fisher, Abbey, Kim, Beth* *yes*

4. What changes are needed in your life to reach the point where you can serve and accept others no matter what their reaction to you might be? *Die to self - to the point where misunderstandings + rejection won't affect me.*

5. What can you do to "put skin on the grace of God" without waiting for others to accept you first? *Go to new people in church + welcome them. Reach out to some who have hurt me.*

6. Are there any trees of bitterness in your life that prevent you from accepting those people whom God accepts? Are there any saplings growing? Prayerfully consider "logging" with Jesus and cutting them down. *thank you Lord for the Makeno, Palmatiers, Andersons, Jacobus' Podvarkas + Millers.*

7. What are the most encouraging things someone could do for you right now? *Love me through my healing. Pray with me + fellowship with me. Help with the many people with needs.*

8. How can you and those in your fellowship nurture a Barnabas-attitude in order to welcome new people? *Always welcome new people + call them 1x/week.*

9. Who are the people in your geographical area (public officials, business people, community and religious leaders) who need encouragement? What specific actions can you take to touch their lives? *School employees librarian, Herta, Helen Golja*

Chapter Four

Riding the Waves of Failure

Can you imagine a surfer trying to dodge the big waves? Though the awesome power of the wave could crush him, the surfer paddles furiously to get into the wave. Success brings one of life's most exhilarating experiences. Failure can be costly. My first experience of surfing was at a place called "The Wedge" in the Newport Beach area of Southern California. Two ocean currents meet at "The Wedge," often resulting in twelve- to fifteen-foot faces on the waves. Body surfers, who do not use surfboards, can get an incredible ride on these monstrous waves. But the power of the wave must not be taken lightly. While we watched, a young man mistimed his takeoff and lost control. We saw him tossed up and then driven under the water. When some friends finally brought him to the surface his body was limp. He was rescued, but his leg was broken, snapped like a stick. I asked my friend, Les, what he thought would happen to the young man. "My best guess is that he'll be back on the beach tomorrow, cast and all. He'll watch others and try to learn how he can get a great ride. Come on, now, Doug, let's give you your first lesson!"

We are all looking for a great ride in life. Great rides, however, only come with great risks. And great risks mean facing the fear of failure. The surfer who goes out into the big waves knows that the wrong position on the wave could result in her tossed around like a ball and then pinned to the bottom, spread-eagled by the force of the current. The fear of failure can be a healthy motive to inspire the surfer to pursue optimum personal conditioning and skill development. But when the fear of failure keeps a capable person out of the water, something has been lost.

In order to experience fully the life God has for us, we must learn to manage the fear of failure. In order to serve God fully in the work of His coming kingdom, we must learn to transform the fear of failure into the energy of obedience. An instructive example of overcoming the fear of failure is Peter's experience of walking on the water. The disciple Peter would learn a lesson of the waves: that taking the risk of failure can be a life-changing step of love and growth. Before we explore Peter's story, we need to understand the magnetic power of our safety zones. This is the power that keeps us on the beach or in the boat. An invisible current of fear often holds us captive, preventing those very steps which we, in our hearts, most desire to take.

I recall leading a youth evangelism team at my home church, College Hill Presbyterian Church in Cincinnati, Ohio. As we began, each of us was eager to share our faith, but none of us felt too secure. On one of the first evenings of calling, we sent out several teams, planning to meet back at the church in two hours, after our visits. When we returned, one team still hadn't arrived. We went through our "debriefing" and closing prayer. As I was walking back into the building after everyone left, one car drove slowly in. It was the other team.

"Hey, guys!" I said as they pulled up, "it must have gone great if you were with them for so long."

The three in the car looked at me without any excitement. Uh-oh, I thought.

"Doug, it didn't go at all. . . ."

"What do you mean?"

"We got to the first home, and we just couldn't get out of the car. So we thought we might feel better if we drove to the second place. . . ." His voice died away.

"So tonight was more of a reconnaissance mission, eh?"

"You could say that—we've gone through more than half a tank of gas!"

"Come on in," I said. "Let's talk this through." These three were embarrassed, and I, to be frank, was disappointed. But as we talked, we had one of the most honest, rich conversations we'd ever had. We discussed our assumptions about how people will react to us (they'd most likely slam the door in our faces!), the questions we are afraid they will ask us ("Why does God allow suffering? Isn't the Bible full of contradictions?"), and the guilt we feel because we know that our walk of faith does not always match our talk ("Oh, yeah, you should talk! I remember when you . . ."). We came to realize that we can only tell the story; we have to trust God to change people's hearts.

When we ended our conversation, a student I'll call Susan said, "Do you think anybody is still awake? I'm ready to visit them now!"

Did that team fail? It looked like it at first. They were too ashamed to meet with the others who had gone out. But the conversation following their "failure" led to fruitful discipleship. We processed some basic issues: the fear of rejection, dealing with the fear of intellectual challenge, and the fear that our walk doesn't match our talk. As a result of that experience, those three team members were able to be more sensitive both in their evangelism calling and in their training of others.

Again and again, we've seen this principle demonstrated: the greatest growth emerges from the soil of failure. We love the growth, but forget the soil, we say. Unless we are "air plants," however, there is very little growth without this soil of failure. Our progress on the voyage of faith means that we will have to deal with the issue of failure, allowing God to transform it into the means of growth. The first step in overcoming this fear is to recognize where it operates in our lives.

Are You Caught in the Force-field of Failure?

The fear of failure keeps many people from doing what they really want to do. The problem is not with a lack of vision. It may not be with a lack of desire. The problem is with an invisible, often ambivalent force of resistance that keeps us captive. We cannot seem to break free to take the step we long to take. I liken this to a magnetic force-field, or to earth's gravitational pull. A spacecraft must exert incredible force to break free of earth's gravity and launch into space. That is how many experience the resistance they feel to taking a risk.

There are at least three force-fields that keep people captive. The first is the fear of what others will think of us. If we set the standard of success as always pleasing others, Jesus' earthly ministry would be labeled a failure. According to John's Gospel, after feeding the 5,000, Jesus taught the crowds that He was "the bread that came down from heaven" (John 6:41). The crowds murmured and mumbled against Him, just like Israel after they were sated with manna. By day's end we read, "From this time many of His disciples turned back and no longer followed Him" (v. 66). Had Jesus failed? Most of us would be quick to justify the sharp decline in the number of Jesus' followers as evidence of His integrity, not a condemnation of poor teaching technique.

Jesus did not fail by God's standards. He was faithful in the teaching of God's truth and in His response to people's needs. Are we able, then, to apply that standard to ourselves when people do not respond to our service? It feels very different when it happens to us!

I was at an annual gathering of pastors with my friend, Steve Hayner, President of Inter-Varsity Christian Fellowship. We were discussing the pressure to please others. "I have to remind myself continually that I live for an audience of one." Steve's words hit home. Live for an audience of one. As Paul writes in Colossians, "Whatever you do, work at it with all your heart, as working for the Lord, not for men, since you know that you will receive an inheritance from the Lord as a reward. It is the Lord Christ you are serving" (Col. 3:23-24).

One of the reasons we may be trying to please others is because we feel judged by them. Who is your judge? Who tells you (whether literally or in your imagination) that you are failing or succeeding? A parent? An influential teacher or coach? Your peers? To what audience are you playing?

Some people have what I call a "critic finder" capacity: they filter out all positive comments and affirmations, dwelling only on their critics and the criticisms that come their way. The result is a low-grade failure-fever. Such people need to learn that criticism is like mud: if you let it dry, it will brush off easily. This is a trained response which can be cultivated with intentional effort. Instead of focusing on the critics, we can cultivate a network of support. Those who are frozen by the fear of failure thaw in the warmth of love and acceptance. One of the most important first steps for breaking free from the force-field of failure is to create a "fail-safe" community. Webster defines fail-safe as "incorporating some feature for automatically counteracting the effect of an anticipated possible source of failure." This is a wonderful metaphor for the fellowship of believers: a place where it is safe to fail.

A second force-field of failure is our fear that we will disappoint God. Our impression of God's standards or demands may intimidate us. I have a close friend who is a very capable preacher. But there was a time when he could hardly endure the agony that came from anticipating the preaching event. The major reason for his struggle was that he never felt his sermon was good enough for God. His fear of failing God almost silenced him! What a loss that would have been. His story is not unique. Many, lay people and clergy alike, have resisted opportunities to serve in the church or in missions because they were afraid, literally, that they were not good enough. The real question, of course, is this: who could ever be good enough? If God depended on perfect people we would still be in Genesis 3!

Third, we may fear that our decisions or actions could cause significant inconvenience to ourselves or others. We are wise to consider carefully the impact of our decisions on our network of relationships. A decision, for example, to uproot a family for a short-term mission project needs the support of the entire family if it is to be fully effective. We need to take seriously Paul's sobering words in 1 Timothy 5:8, "If anyone does not provide for his relatives, and especially for his immediate family, he has denied the faith and is worse than an unbeliever." Having said this, there are times when a diligent search of our hearts is required to determine if we are really caring for our loved ones, or hiding behind them. It may be that the Lord is calling us to take a great risk that will challenge the significant people in our lives to see God work in new, life-enlarging ways.

The fear of failure, whatever its source, makes us more vulnerable to failure. The skater who falls attempting a difficult triple axel jump may become preoccupied with the fall instead of visualizing the successful accomplishment. The solution is to learn from the fear, then turn from it and focus on the goal.

The fear of failure robs us of tapping the deepest riches of life. Riches aren't mined on the surface. They require the risk of going deeper, of exploring uncharted territory, of "wasting time and resources" learning what doesn't work. The creative process of exploration can appear to be an extravagant waste—until we strike gold. Then all the effort pales in comparison to the benefits. We need the courage to risk exploration. Start by telling yourself there are no guarantees of success. The only guarantee in life is that of the boredom, dullness, and tepidity of a safe life.

We begin, then, with the soul-searching task of exploring our "failure-sensitive areas." Which of the three force-fields most affect your life? In what specific areas: your job? your schooling? your friendships or marriage? your family? your moral behavior? Once we have inventoried these, we need to reexamine our assumptions about success and failure. This will prepare us to face failure straight on.

Replace a Failure Mentality with a Faithfulness Mentality

The intimidating power of failure is fueled by unbiblical definitions of success. When we define success as never doing wrong, never making a bad decision, or always meeting our highest expectations, we are set for a big fall. Success for a follower of Jesus Christ is seen in the act of obedience, not in the results. Results provide feedback on our decisions and actions. They help us understand whether a particular choice was appropriate or productive for a particular circumstance. But every situation involves countless variables and dynamics beyond our control. We may use our best judgment, but we cannot control how others will respond to our decision. Results, therefore, are not criteria for determining our personal worth and character.

Successful results do not define us. We are defined by faith. Success is a category of experience independent of our being. A biblical view of success means that failure doesn't tell us who we are; it is feedback on how we are doing. This perspective does not remove the motivation nor the responsibility to be faithful disciples and diligent stewards of the gifts God has given us. But it frees us to focus on the primacy of our love for God and our acts of obedience, instead of on fulfilling spiritual "sales quotas." We can risk failure because we are not risking our identity.

Did it ever appear to you that God is not as impressed with success as human logic would seem to dictate? In Deuteronomy 7 we read, "The Lord did not set His affection on you and choose you because you were more numerous than other peoples, for you were the fewest of all peoples. But it was because the Lord loved you" (Deut. 7:7-8). God is not impressed with numbers, credentials, or accomplishments, but with faith and faithfulness. His purpose is to display His grace and mercy in our lives. Ironically, our "success" could become a barrier to His blessing! It could deceive us into self-reliance and complacency. Failure, on the other hand, can be the doorway to a deeper life.

The opposite of failure is not success; it is faithfulness rooted in God's power and direction. Failure is a criteria which measures outward results; faithfulness is a quality of the heart which provides the climate for growth. Failure judges a person without mercy or empathy for the difficulties of life; faithfulness nurtures a person on the voyage of spiritual formation and risk-taking. Failure looks at the immediate; faithfulness draws courage from the long-range view. Failure says, "Forget it!" while faithfulness says, "How can I do this with the strength God mightily inspires within me?" Failure is a judgment; faithfulness is promise.

The most helpful principle for nurturing a faith mentality is to view results in terms of "fruit." Fruit is the natural product of a healthy vine or tree. The psalmist celebrates the promise of the blessed person who delights in the Lord. "He is like a tree planted by streams of water, which yields its fruit in season" (Ps. 1:3). There are a variety of fruit trees which yield different types of fruit in different seasons. Citrus trees and apple trees are different. They cannot be judged at the same time, nor with the same criteria. Likewise, each of us is a different type of tree in the orchard of God. We will not bear fruit in every season, nor will we always look successful. The important thing is that we are delighting in the Lord.

Jesus taught this clearly in John 15:5, "I am the vine; you are the branches. If a man [or woman] remains in Me and I in him, he will bear much fruit; apart from Me you can do nothing" (John 15:5). My friend and mentor, Dr. Bob Munger, has a short-hand formula for this verse: $10 \times 0 = 0$. In other words, no amount of effort on our part (the "10") will result in any lasting fruit if we fail to abide in Christ ("times 0"). When we fail to abide, neglecting to tap the vital power of the Holy Spirit dwelling within us, we are tempted to lead a safe life. At the end of the day, what will we have to show for it? No scars, but also no stories! No significant losses, but no significant gains!

The inverse is also true: if we abide in Christ, we will bear fruit that will last. "You did not choose Me, but I chose you to go and bear fruit—fruit that will last" (John 15:16). Our faith is expressed in the fruit we yield. That fruit emerges naturally from our roots in Christ.

When we operate out of a success mentality, we ask questions such as: How many people were present? How much did we sell? How are we doing in the ratings? What do "the important people" think of us? How many responded to us? Did the person pray with us to accept Jesus Christ? Were we rejected? These questions have a place in our growth and evaluations of our career, our relationships, or our ministry. But if we use them as the primary basis for determining our faithfulness in God's eyes, we have missed the biblical message.

I'm convinced that many things we label as failures are, in fact, honorable, though immature fruit. Because so many factors are beyond our control, we are unwise and unrealistic when we hold ourselves accountable for results where we have no control.

Likewise, much of what we label success may not be viewed that way in light of the kingdom. Jesus' unsettling words in Matthew 7 are addressed to some people who had apparently been quite successful according to their own standards. Jesus said,

> Not everyone who says to Me, "Lord, Lord," will enter the kingdom of heaven, but only he who does the will of My Father who is in heaven. Many will say to Me on that day, "Lord, Lord, did we not prophesy in

Your name, and in Your name drive out demons and
perform many miracles?" Then I will tell them plainly,
"I never knew you. Away from Me, you evildoers!"
(Matt. 7:21-23)

When we move from an external measurement of success to
an internal measure, we begin to understand that success has
much more to do with motivation and direction, than with
achievement and destination. The motivational speaker Earl
Nightingale defines success as, "The progressive realization of
a worthy ideal."[1] Denis Waitley works with this definition and
develops it more fully, "Total success is the continuing involvement in the pursuit of a worthy ideal, which is being
realized for the benefit of others—rather than at their expense."[2] My personal definition of success is this: Success is
the active pursuit of God's ideal for life and character, through
the power of the Holy Spirit, bearing fruit for God's glory. No
one definition can capture what may be essential to you, so I
suggest you write your own definition.

The essential point of these definitions is that success is
defined in terms of faithfulness to personal responsibility, re-
gardless of actual accomplishments. Success is a process, not a
product. It is determined by character, not by calculations. It
is progressive, not finite. This gives us hope because we cannot
control how people react to us. I cannot, for example, control
whether or not this book becomes a bestseller. But I am successful if I have honored the Lord and His people in the
attempt. The results will take care of themselves. Paul highlights this principle when he reminds us, "I planted the seed,
Apollos watered it, but God made it grow" (1 Cor. 3:6). The
genuine "success questions" are these: were we faithful in
planting when God gave the opportunity? Were we faithful in
watering and cultivating the seeds God provided? That's all we
can control. Only God controls the soil and germination. Our
success is in scattering the seed through proclamation and service and in watering the seed with prayer and compassionate
attention.

I would suggest a different set of questions as a test for
evaluating the fruit and faithfulness of our lives. These are

geared to inner dynamics of spirit and character, not to the outer criteria of results and measurements. The questions are: Does this thought, action, or decision honor God? Does it honor the principles of God's Word? Does it honor others for whom it is intended? Does it honor my gifts and stewardship? Am I "walking in the light" in terms of my motives and conduct as I pursue this goal? With a faithfulness mentality, we still give our best effort, but our primary focus is on the Lord, not the situation.

New freedom and joy enter our lives when our actions are viewed from the perspective of faithfulness and fruit. We gain the freedom to dream again, to take daring steps of faith. *To risk failure on the voyage of faith is one of the clearest expressions of our love and commitment to the Lord.* To risk failure does not drive God from us; it draws God to us.

There is no greater failure than refusing to do what the Lord is stirring your heart to do. It is tragic when God invites us to test the infinite resources of faith, but we refuse to step out. We have often heard that we need to get out of our comfort zones in order to do God's work. On the subject of failure, we need to get out of our safety zones. Our "safety zones" are places of predictability. In our safety zones, we do not have to cope with surprises which require improvisation. We are soothed by the routine. Life in the safety zone does not demand much of us. We can cruise on autopilot. Life may not be rewarding, but that's fine because neither is it taxing. The overriding value is security. The overwhelming result? Boredom! A tasteless faith.

The disciple Peter had a faithfulness mentality, even when his faith was in its embryonic stages. Consequently, he had some of life's most exhilarating experiences. But they were not without risk, not without failure.

Risk a Walk on the Waves

In Matthew 14:22-33, we read the account of Jesus walking across the water and Peter asking to walk on the water with Him. In this situation, Peter moves from the safety zone of untested faith into the adventure arena of testing his faith. The word "testing" may make some uncomfortable because we know the verse which says, "Do not put the Lord your God to the test" (Matt. 4:7, citing Deut. 6:16). This refers to the sinful sense of testing. The sinful form of testing, which Jesus resisted in the wilderness, meant putting God's promises to the test with random, capricious acts of daring or danger (see Matt. 4). Peter's test, on the other hand, is that of testing his faith by exploring the nature of God's resources.

It was predawn. The previous day the disciples had witnessed one of Jesus' most dramatic miracles, the feeding of over 5,000 men, women, and children. After the disciples had gathered twelve basketfuls of broken pieces (one for each of them!), Jesus sent them in a boat to the other side of the lake. Meanwhile, He dismissed the crowd, continuing to minister to them. Having fed the people, Jesus withdrew to feed His own soul. He went up on a mountainside to pray. We can only speculate, but passages such as John 6 would suggest that He prayed that the people would understand that He was the living, new manna of God, the bread which could nourish the deepest hunger of their souls. He knew they were more interested in the physical bread He could provide, than the spiritual nourishment He promised. In spite of the risk of being misunderstood, however, He fed their bodies, taught their minds, and prayed for their souls.

Then, a practical problem arose: the disciples had the boat, but Jesus was on the shore. It was a long walk around the lake. How would Jesus reunite with the disciples? Jesus found a creative solution: walking across the water as if it were land. Many people, including scholars, struggle with this miracle because it is different in character from Jesus' other miracles. His other miracles were normally conducted to save people or to help them.[3] In this case, the disciples are struggling in the wind and the waves, but they do not seem to be in imminent danger. Jesus' action looks like a "miracle of convenience." He had done nothing like this before, and nothing like it afterward. How do we explain this?

The objections to this miracle do not dissuade me. I see this miracle, in part, as a wonderful picture of Jesus meeting practical necessity in a delightful, exhilarating manner. The strict "usefulness code" that scholars discern in Jesus' modus operandi for miracles need not become a restrictive criteria for the Lord God Almighty! I have a problem with those who have a problem with the Lord Almighty doing whatever He wants! He will not fit the consistency of our analysis. The Savior did this as a response to His own need. It brought glory to God. We must humble ourselves before His wonders. This is not to say that God is in "the miracle business," performing the equivalent of spiritual circus acts. I merely mean that we have crossed over into precarious presumption when we judge this miracle as unfitting of Jesus Christ.

It may help us to realize that the disciples were the first skeptics. When they first saw Jesus walking on the water, they were terrified. "It's a ghost!" they said, crying out in fear. They failed to recognize the Lord, shaken by the unexpected. Jesus' response was one of calm assurance: "Take courage! It is I. Don't be afraid."

Jesus' first command stops fear in its icy tracks. If courage is commanded, we must believe it is possible. This may be news to us. We tend to think that courage is a feeling beyond our control. In fact, it is the heart's response to our perception of a situation. If we can view the situation from God's perspective, with the assurance of His presence, courage will arise within us. The Lord gave a similar command to Joshua when he assumed leadership following the death of Moses. "Have I not commanded you? Be strong and courageous. Do not be terrified; do not be discouraged, for the Lord your God will be with you wherever you go" (Josh. 1:9).

Jesus then gave the basis for his command, "It is I." We could translate, "It is I," as "I am!" The Greek term, *ego eimi*, is not just an announcement of presence. It is a "divine Self-revelation," based on God's revealed name to Moses in Exodus 3.[4] Our courage is rooted in Jesus' identity as God, not in denial or wishful thinking.

As the disciples are attempting to make sense of this encounter, Peter makes a bold request. He is intrigued by a fascinating opportunity. He was attracted by God's love and power. Not everyone agrees with this interpretation, however. Some biblical commentators view Peter in a critical light, accusing him of impulsive, arrogant presumption. John Calvin (with whom I rarely differ!) wrote that "by this example believers are taught to beware of over-much rashness . . . of transgressing . . . limits."[5] His view is that Peter well-deserved to sink, because God does not want us to attempt such things.

I take a much more sympathetic view. Was the Lord more pleased with Peter getting out of the boat, or the disciples who stayed in the boat? If Jesus was displeased with Peter, why did He command him to come? Was He being cruel, setting Peter up for failure or rebuke? Those who assert this must consider the implications of Jesus deliberately putting a person at risk, like an antagonist.

Peter's request was a sign of love and commitment, which Jesus received as such. His desire overrode all caution. Peter was willing to take a risk few of us can ever imagine in order to be closer to Jesus. We must note the significance of "coming to Christ on the water." Even when we risk, we are walking to and with Christ in every situation. We are getting out of our safety zones in order to be closer to Him. Peter wanted to join in the wonder of the Lord's work. This was more than a request to have some fun.

Initially, Peter succeeded. He walked on water! This is truly astounding. What must it have been like to feel the surging waves beneath his feet? What was it like to sense the support of a power that carried him above the awe-full power of the sea? Peter was walking as in a dream, focusing intensely on Jesus. Then, a strong wind distracted him. He looked around and must have said, "What am I doing?" His heart became heavy with fear—and so did he. He began to sink, the Bible tells us. How long, exactly, does it take for us to *begin* to sink and *completely* sink? A split second! We're not talking about a long time here! Peter just had time to scream, "Lord, save me," before he was going under the waves. Immediately, Jesus saved him.

I have often wondered: how did Peter and Jesus arrive at the boat? Did Jesus carry Peter? Did they swim back? Did Peter swim while Jesus walked? The Bible gives us no clue. My own opinion: I think Peter walked back, leaning on Jesus. The reason I say this is that Jesus speaks to Peter *before* they get back into the boat. "You of little faith. Why did you doubt?" Many people take the Lord's words to Peter as a stern rebuke of Peter's failure. Again, I think there is a different message here.

I recall watching the coach of a high-diving student as they worked out at a swim club. The diver almost completed the twist and rotation for a two-and-one-half dive with a full twist, but opened too soon at the end. A resounding "smack" told everyone in the area that someone was hurting.

"You almost made it. What happened?"

"I lost confidence," gasped the diver, trying to manage the stinging pain. "It was all working so well that I really couldn't believe it! I got scared and lost concentration."

"Why did you lose confidence? You can do it; you really can! Now, get back up there and go for it!"

The coach was not scolding the diver. She was encouraging him. She knew that the ability of the diver and the technique of her instruction could come together if the diver would believe and follow through.

Walking on water is far different from diving into it. Peter did not possess the power within himself as a human being to walk on water. No amount of concentration, willpower, or possibility thinking could bring about such a miracle. Nevertheless, there is a lesson we can learn from the coach: When we experience pain because of failure, we are often on the very brink of success. What others view as failure is really the experience of going deeper, reaching higher, traveling farther on the road to meaningful achievement.

I'll bet the guys in the boat envied Peter. Sure, some were glad they hadn't put themselves in that awkward situation. How sad! For though Peter "failed," he had the experience of a lifetime—and a lifetime to learn that growth takes place at the edge of risk. When he spoke on that first Pentecost morning, he stepped out of the boat again—and this time he made it all the way! I believe Peter's courage in the early church was the fruit of this time of sinking.

Peter's ride on the wave of failure taught him at least three very significant lessons. First, he learned the lesson of God's reliable presence. He could rely on the Lord in his greatest need. He now knew clearly that God doesn't desert a person who has gone out on a limb for Him. Second, he learned the lesson of his own frailty. He had a vivid understanding of human vulnerability. Like Peter, when we get out of the boat, we quickly find that our own ingenuity is hopeless against the wind and waves. That brings the joy of the third lesson: We gain a greater understanding of God's resources. He immediately reaches out with a strong hand to save us.

What Do We Do When We Truly Fail the Lord and Others?

The model of 1 John 2:1-2 helps us, "I write this to you so that you will not sin. But if anybody does sin, we have One who speaks to the Father in our defense—Jesus Christ, the Righteous One. He is the atoning sacrifice for our sins, and not only for ours but also for the sins of the whole world." We want to urge people to do everything possible to seek faithfulness. But if they do fail, there is a remedy. Failure is not fatal.

The most helpful counsel I've encountered on this subject comes from the writings of Fenelon, a spiritual director in the seventeenth century, in the time of Louis XIV of France. Among his many wise counsels on imperfection, he wrote:

> Do not be overly concerned about your defects. Instead concentrate on having an unceasing love for Jesus, and you shall be much forgiven because you have loved much.... When we look at our defects in peace through the spirit of Jesus, they vanish before the majesty of His love. But when we concentrate on our defects, forgetting that Jesus loves us, we become restless, the presence of God is interrupted, and the flow of God's love is hindered. The humiliation we feel about our own defects can often be a greater fault than the original defect itself if it keeps you from moving into the realization of God's love.[6]

When we fall, we fall to our knees. We are not to wallow in pity, seeking to atone for our sin through the misery of our guilt. We have just learned once again the reason for the cross and the empty tomb.

Getting Out of Our Boats

If the people of God in the church of Jesus Christ are to participate in the coming kingdom, we are going to have to try new ways, welcome new cultures, risk new formats, and use new, new methods to communicate the old, old story. There are likely to be many failures, but they can be glorious ones. The church fails not because arguments against the Gospel are so strong, but because our willingness to risk is so weak.

For me, one area of getting out of the boat and onto the waves has been in the area of seeking health and healing in obedience to Christ's command. I have consistently taken the model of Jesus seriously: "Jesus went throughout Galilee, teaching in their synagogues, preaching the good news of the kingdom, and healing every disease and sickness among the people" (Matt. 4:23). His ministry was balanced with teaching, preaching, and healing. He brought the grace and power of God to the mind, heart, and body. The fact is, however, that most of us are more comfortable ministering to the mind and heart than trusting God to heal the body.

I have been convicted to get out of the boat and invite our congregation to pray for healing and see what God will do. The following testimony comes from a member of my congregation, and shared here with her permission. Jan tells about a glorious ride on the waves. She writes:

At about the age of thirty (1970) I began to have some aches and pains in my joints. On some days they would be quite uncomfortable, and on other days they would be barely discernible. It was more of a bother than a concern at that time. After a couple of years of this, I mentioned it to my elderly doctor who had been our family physician since my childhood. He knew our whole family. He diagnosed arthritis, of course. "You've got so much of it in your family that you shouldn't be surprised. And don't forget, you had rheumatic fever at age five. That's a contributing factor. We'll just pray that it's osteo and not rheumatoid."

As time went on the aches and pains got worse and

worse, and I had more and more uncomfortable days. During this time I began to ask God what I should be learning from Him about this. "Lord, I know there is a huge lesson here. What is it?" I didn't get a clear answer. I had to be *patient*.

About 1980 our physician retired, and we found a new one. I was feeling pretty bad by that time. I told him that not only did my joints hurt, but so did my muscles. He did a series of tests and informed me that I had not just osteo and rheumatoid arthritis, but that I also had chronic fibromyalgia. Simply put, that is a rheumatoid disease that attacks the muscles. He informed me too that all of my joints were affected with arthritis and all of my muscles were affected with fibromyalgia. Most doctors don't know a lot about fibromyalgia, but his wife has it so he has done extra study on it.

On most days I felt like a person with old-fashioned achy flu. I would ache all over, but I had no fever. I wasn't ill. The doctor began to prescribe medications. I started with nonsteroidal anti-inflammatory drugs and pain medication. As time went by we kept changing both medications to stronger and stronger drugs. Later we added a sleeping medication. Naturally, there were side effects to these drugs. I tried to do without the medication several times, but I would be in tears from the pain.

Through all of this I was continually praying, "Lord, make it clear what You want me to know from You, and then take this disease away." And God said, "Wait. Have *patience.*"

Just before September 1991, I was in bad shape. I knew I was going to have to take some time off work. I didn't know if it would be several months or the rest of my life. My left arm and hand were in constant, heavy-duty pain, and I'm left-handed. I was doing all of my paperwork with my right hand, which was very slow. It was very painful to write on the chalkboard. The rest of my body was giving me fits too.

I couldn't sleep well at night. One of the symptoms of fibromyalgia is an inability to get into REM sleep, so I had constant sleep deprivation. That brought about another symptom: chronic fatigue. I was a person living with pain and exhaustion.

Bob and I had talked about going to a healing service at another church, because we didn't think Presbyterians would do it. Then you presented your healing experience. That's when Bob asked you if we could come together to pray for my healing. We did so on September 29, 1991.

During that hour I felt the strong presence of the Spirit of God, especially when you prayed for the Holy Spirit to come with *more power* and *more power!* I felt great warmth was going into my body and radiating from it.

Afterward, I had some immediate changes. I could bend and twist, and my arm was about 60% improved. Each day it was easier and easier to get up, easier to move, and I slept! At the end of the week I felt like a new person! I stopped all medication on the day of prayer. I had no need of it. My doctor examined me and confirmed that I no longer need medication. God had chosen to heal me that day!

I continue to praise Him and thank Him! My mountain has been moved by Him! It has been a monumental and a humbling experience. The Lord changed my life!

Thank You, Jesus, for giving me the faith to be healed! Thank You for friends and family that pray. Thank You for a pastor that is strong in Your word. And thank You, Lord, for miracles!

Any who have begun to step out of the boat in the area of healing prayer know that there are many times your head gets wet! But times such as this, when the Lord reaches out in mercy, are beyond comparison.

Getting out of the boat happens in less dramatic, but still meaningful ways. In our congregation, we have begun taking "prayer walks" through the neighborhoods surrounding our downtown church. A team of two or three people simply stroll down the sidewalk, praying for the people in the homes they pass, the children on the playground, the businesses in the area. The first steps are intimidating. But the encouragement of the group and the sense that God is pleased bring strength and courage. Some of our teams have greeted people who are outside and begun conversations with them. When they ask the people, "Is there any way we can pray for you?" the responses are often very positive. People have been surprisingly open and appreciative.

My wife, Sarah, has begun to take the risk of sharing poems she has written for people out of her intercessory prayer. She felt foolish at the risk of sharing these with others. "What if my poems aren't good?" she'd ask me. I honestly believe her poems are good, but more special to me was the love and wisdom they expressed. Sarah's risk of sharing herself has resulted in something more than appreciation of her poetic ability. The love behind her poems carries the message of God's love past all kinds of barriers, right into people's hearts. Not only is her creativity beginning to flourish because she has gotten out of the boat, but her ministry has as well.

I remember Lloyd Ogilvie asking the question, "If you had no fear of failure, what would you attempt for God?" For some, it might mean daring to step into a new area of ministry. For others, it could be making contact with people in new ways. For you—well, what does it mean to you? When this attitude gets hold of us, the people of God are going to unlock a joy and a power that cannot help but bear fruit. *To risk failure on the voyage of faith is one of the clearest expressions of our love and commitment to the Lord.* May God help us get out of the boat. Here's to a great ride!

Investing in Your "R & D"
Questions for Reflection and Discussion

1. What is the failure you most fear? (You may want to put these in rank order from most fearful [#1] to least fearful.)
   ____ a. Losing your job
   ____ b. Losing your marriage
   ____ c. Moral failure
   _1_ d. Failing as a parent
   _3_ e. Financial failure
   ____ f. Failure of a project at work
   _2_ g. Other _ministry (dance)_
   ____ h. I honestly do not fear failure

2. What force-field of failure affects you the most?
   _1_ a. What others think
   ____ b. That we might disappoint God
   ____ c. That we will cause significant inconvenience to ourselves or others

3. In what areas of your life would others see you as success-ful? Has this success ever been a block or hindrance to your relationship to God? *Being a nice person - tight with leadership - no - but perhaps open to more criticism*

4. Have any failures in your life opened doors: *Closer to Him in Crisis*
   _✓_ a. To a greater sense of God's presence? Explain.
   _✓_ b. To a greater appreciation of your own vulnerability? Explain. *points me more to depend on God*
   _✓_ c. To a greater understanding of God's resources? Explain. *His peace that we can't understand*

5. Do you have a judge? Does someone tell you (literally or in your imagination) that you are failing or succeeding? *Yes, some people have said "we are watching you"*

6. Do you think you have a "critic finder" capacity? How does this affect your ability to handle risk and failure? *Yes adds to anxiety*

7. Do you feel you operate more out of a success mentality or a faithfulness mentality? How would you like to change? *Faithfulness*

8. Write your own definition of success.

To please God, Trust & obey

9. Describe a time when you were faithful in planting, watering, or cultivating, even though the results were less than what had been hoped. ~~Eat~~ *a person (two)*

organize a
Prayer
walks

10. How do you respond to Lloyd Ogilvie's question, "If you had no fear of failure, what would you attempt for God?"

Teach ~~others~~ at meetings more often —
~~be more vulnerable~~

11. How is God inviting you to get out of the boat?

or
Praise
Parade

Trust me — Obey me — look
only to me — I'll take
care of the Peters & Judas'
+ Sanhedrins — you
look to me.

Chapter Five

Forsaking
Fear-formed Idols

A famous comedian used to get great laughs when he said, "The devil made me do it!" It seems funny to blame someone else for our failings. But the devil isn't the only one who gets the blame. There have been too many times in history when a chill runs down our spines as some deranged person says, "The Lord made me do it." The murder of a doctor at an abortion clinic by one who says she was obeying the Lord; the Reverend Jim Jones telling his religious followers at a compound in Guyana that, in the name of God, they should drink poisoned Kool-Aid; religious leader David Koresh commanding his followers to fight the "enemies of the faith," referring to the United States government, in an apocalyptic battle in Waco, Texas—these are all events justified in the name of God. What kind of God?

Far from being irrelevant, our ideas about God can have a determining influence on our lives. A.W. Tozer wrote,

> What comes to our minds when we think about God is the most important thing about us ... and the most portentous fact about any man is not what he at a given time may say or do, but what he in his deep heart conceives God to be like. *We tend by a secret law of the soul to move toward our mental image of God.*[1]

When asked what they think of God, it is not unusual to find people who have an unhealthy fear of God. I remember counseling with a man who had recently professed faith in Christ. He was a successful young man, moving to the top of his field in the media, happily married with young children. In many ways, he struck me as one who "had it made." In the course of our discussion, he said, "Doug, I have to tell you something; it's one of the most embarrassing things in my life."

Naturally, my mind began to race over the all-too-familiar ground of "embarrassing things" I have heard before. But I wasn't ready for this one.

"I am terrified of Communion. When they pass the tray to me, my hands shake so that I almost spill the juice. My mouth is like cotton; it's all I can do to keep from running out of the sanctuary."

He had grown up in a highly liturgical church. As a young boy he had been deeply impressed but frightened by the language of sin and death and blood and judgment that are part of the drama of the Eucharist. Even after experiencing Christ anew, the "awe-fullness" of the Lord's Table was too much for him. He was frightened by a soul-shaking sense of the justice and holiness of God which somehow blinded him to the central message of mercy. We talked on several occasions, but it was a slow journey out of fear for him.

The Book of Proverbs says, "The fear of the Lord is the beginning of knowledge" (Prov. 1:7), but for many it is the start of confusion. How can we love that which we fear? How can we fear that which we love? This confusion is much more than an intellectual matter, to be handled at a convenient time when we have nothing else pressing. As Tozer comments, our view of God greatly influences our fundamental view of life and of ourselves. If we are to live fully and faithfully, we must know God truly, perceiving God's nature and work as accurately as possible in this life.

Knowing God the way God truly is, however, is not the norm, even among believers. Painful experiences and poor education in biblical truth have resulted in the shaping of distorted concepts formed more by fear than by faith. These fear-formed idols can block our spiritual progress, prevent a deepening fellowship with God, and derail our attempts to serve God.

A Case of Misrepresentation

It was the first day of my "Introduction to Philosophy" class at the university. "My job," said the professor, "is to force you to question everything you ever believed." In that environment, that was a destructive challenge, sending many students into spiritual shock. But in one sense, this is a task all of us should undertake. Unconsciously, we have formed images of God which are inaccurate and unworthy of His name and glory. These images—I dare to call them idols—need not be seen as malicious sins of commission. They are not necessarily intentional acts of idol-making. But they can have the effect of distorting, disrupting, and devaluing our relationship with the Lord.

How can you know if you have some fear-formed idols? I would suggest that you can test yourself with a few diagnostic questions. Ask yourself:

1. "What are the first thoughts that come to mind when I think of the Lord? Do these thoughts draw me closer to God and encourage me as a person? Or do I feel resistant to God and uncomfortable at the thought of drawing closer?"
2. "What characteristics of God are most important to me? Where did I develop my concept of these characteristics? From the Bible or from my experience?"
3. "How do I respond when I hear teaching on the grace and goodness of God? Do I celebrate God, or find myself waging an inner battle with resentment toward God?"

Now, before you get discouraged and lay this chapter down, let me invite you to walk with me as one who is learning that a proper knowledge of God bears the fruit of love, joy, and peace in the most practical ways. When we truly understand

God, we understand the words of the psalmist, "Taste and see that the Lord is good" (Ps. 34:8). It is a joy to know God, satisfying to serve God, energizing to worship God, intriguing to search the mind of God, and fulfilling to be quiet in God's presence. If this is not your experience, then this search could literally transform your life—if not in a moment, then over the course of a brief time.

There's nothing much more frustrating than being misrepresented by or to another person. When our motives are questioned, or our actions are misinterpreted and misunderstood, we do everything in our power to set the record straight. We want to be known for who we are, not for what other people mis-think we are. We want to be accepted "in our own image," not created "in the image" of another's imagination.

This is true of God. The central temptation of religious instinct has been to fashion God according to our own specifications or according to our own experience. To twist the familiar words of Genesis, we might say that from the beginning, man and woman have been tempted to create God in their own image.

At least two primary forces conspire to shape inadequate and negative images of God. The first is that of limited human reasoning. We have developed distorted images of God because we have tried to reason our way to a concept of God with flawed human logic. We are faced with a basic philosophical problem: how can a finite, time-limited person hope to comprehend the infinite, timeless Author of life? How can a mortal person ever hope to comprehend the eternal God? As well might an ant write a dissertation on the nature of human love! We are like people with no eyes, standing blindfolded in a dark room in the middle of the night, being asked to describe the visual facts of a sunrise we have never seen. We may offer our best speculation based on our own experience or imagination, but it will, by definition, be inadequate because we are extremely limited in these matters.

Human logic can discern some of the characteristics of a Creator, but they will be incomplete and "out of context," lacking a consistent and adequate frame of reference. For example, the splendor of the snowcapped mountains which speak to some of the majesty of God can be a curse to those who must cross them in winter. The order and harmony of the creation on a sunny day seems to be mockery on the day of the hurricane. There are multiple meanings in every situation. We need more than that which our observations provide in order to determine the true nature of God.

The second factor which contributes to inadequate and negative images of God is that of our limited experience, and especially our experiences of being wounded and being a wounding people. Our pain and disappointments grind distorted lenses through which we try to envision the "Supreme Being." Our sense of "what is true" cannot stand in isolation from our experience. Truth can, in fact, overcome the limitations of our experience, but it must first confront that experience. Think of the primitive people who truly believe that the sun rises and sets every day. They can be brought to the place of understanding the facts of astronomy, but only by the demonstration of a truth which explains their experience and puts it in a larger context.

This second factor, the "personal experience factor," is crucial to understand. Many people have a difficult time entering into an intimate relationship with God because they have suffered violations of intimacy in their significant relationships. If you have been attacked and bitten by a dog, you may well have a difficult time with all dogs. If you have been abused by one from whom you expected love, you may resist trusting yourself to love and be loved by any who say they love you.

This contributes to one of the raging debates in theology today concerning "God language," especially gender language used to describe God, such as "God the Father." One of the primary arguments that some bring against the use of the term "Father," a term that is central to biblical revelation, is that it limits our concept of God, especially for those who have suffered at the hands of a less-than-adequate or even abusive father. We can agree that the concept of God in Scripture is much richer than many have portrayed. For instance, God demonstrates characteristics that we normally indicate as feminine, such as tenderness and nurture. A classic reference is from Isaiah, "Can a mother forget the baby at her breast and have no compassion on the child she has borne? Though she may forget, I will not forget you!" (Isa. 49:15)

We encounter significant problems, however, by "feminizing" God at the expense of "de-masculinizing" God. While this is a very complex topic, we need to understand that the revelation of God as Father is meant to define and establish the standards for our concept of fatherhood, not vice-versa (see Eph. 4:14-15). God is not defined by our experience, but the reverse is to be the case. The reality of God is meant both to correct that which we have misunderstood and to heal that which we have suffered. The entire process of redemption is meant to touch and transform life by redefinition in the light of revelation in Jesus Christ.

The new creation in Christ (see 2 Cor. 5:17) is necessary because the categories of the old creation have been not only distorted, but totally perverted from God's original design. When we define God solely or primarily by our experience in life, we limit God to the consequences of our sin. It would be like prohibiting all further space exploration because of the explosion of the space shuttle *Challenger*, which resulted in the death of the entire crew. The proper response is not to surrender to the pain, but to rise above it through the noble pursuit of truth.

I realize that this is "heavy" material, but these problems are touching the everyday lives of ordinary people. Our failure to think them through clearly is leading to such confusion that significant numbers of congregations and denominations are caught in a maelstrom of conflict. When our image of God is determined by our sense of guilt, by our experience of betrayal, by our fear, by our grief, or by any other experience, we will wander into a barren wasteland. Flawed thinking leads to flawed perception, and flawed perceptions lead to unhealthy relationships. Nowhere is this more tragic than in our relationship with God.

What are some of the common fear-formed idols that vie for our worship? You will want to develop your own list, but here are four that I have frequently encountered.

The Deal-Maker. The Deal-Maker god wants to take advantage of us, using his position of power to secure things from us. People who serve the Deal-Maker approach prayer as a business deal, carefully negotiating and bargaining for what they hope to secure from Deal-Maker. Worship is a business transaction, offerings are a down payment, and service is a bargaining chit. Just stating this position reveals its shortcomings and absurdity. If God is God, then what could a human being possibly offer that God couldn't create for Himself?

The Angry One is the god who is resentful of us and must be cajoled and placated to give us what we need or desire. This god is more concerned with getting even than with maintaining a relationship. People who serve this idol live in the fear of offending god. How close can you get to an angry person? You can possibly respect a person who has high standards. You may try not to offend them, but you cannot draw close to them. The situation, at best, is one of peaceful coexistence, characterized by emotional distance and coolness.

The Busy One is the god who is preoccupied with more important things in the universe, but will give us occasional attention. I call this "god behind the newspaper," like the parent who keeps reading the paper, saying, "Uh-huh, uh-huh," to a child who is telling a story. This is an idol, an unconcerned god, like the deistic view of God, who started everything in motion. Now that the universe is ticking away, this god has better things to do than worry about the little things that bother us.

The Demanding One is hooked on perfection and expects us to meet impossible standards. This idol is like the sport coach who never gives a compliment, but keeps setting the performance mark higher and higher. The Demanding One wants to deny us any fun.

There are many other gods in the panoply of fear-formed idols, but I have said enough to make the point that human logic and experience are most likely to lead us away from a true knowledge of God.

Living with an Unhealthy Fear of God

What is the impact of misunderstanding the nature of God? The first consequence is a loss of connection. Having an unhealthy fear of God disrupts our relationship with God. In fact, I have come to believe that the fundamental principle behind the prohibition of idolatry is God's desire to prevent this loss of connection. God is not threatened by idols, as if they could diminish His power. He does not want to share His glory with another, but we realize that an idol is powerless to detract one iota of glory from God. God's prohibition against idolatry arises primarily from the fact that it cheats us and distorts our fellowship with God.

Why does God say, "You shall have no other gods before Me. You shall not make for yourself an idol"? (Ex. 20:3-4) The reason is given in verse 5, "For I, the Lord your God, am a jealous God." Jealousy is an essential word in the vocabulary of love. This term addresses our relationship with the Lord more than it addresses God's desire to preserve His own reputation. The "green-eyed monster jealousy," which refers to unhealthy suspicion and possessiveness, is not intended here.

In his classic book, *Knowing God*, J.I. Packer writes, "But there is another sort of jealousy—zeal to protect a love-relationship, or to avenge it when broken. . . . This sort of jealousy is a positive virtue."[2] This resolve to protect the relationship is one of the primary expressions of valuing it. God's relationship to His people is likened to a marriage covenant. As such, this holy jealousy reflects the healthy desire to preserve the appropriate boundaries of love and devotion which are part of the sacred oneness of the covenant. God wants our full devotion, even as a spouse wants the undivided loyalty of the marriage partner. God is jealous for us to be free from fear so that we can be free to love God and to live joyfully without the barriers of intimidation and misunderstanding.

A second consequence of an unhealthy fear of God is a loss of confidence in the resources of God. The power of God is closely linked with the justice and character of God. A god created in our image is a god incapable of dealing with our problems. We want a god who is easy enough for us to please but strong enough to perform. When we emphasize one aspect over another, we get neither. If we attempt to dilute the majesty of God which intimidates us, we weaken the power of that which liberates us. On the other hand, being intimidated by

His power dissuades us from seeking support from Him.

The third consequence is what we might call a "loss of compass," or a sense of disorientation which leaves us wandering with questions of purpose and meaning. This has a corrosive effect on our spiritual lives. Paul describes it as receiving in our nature the penalty for our perversions (see Rom. 1:27). This is strong language and should be applied with the understanding that these consequences vary in their intensity, depending on our response to or rejection of God. Our view of God is reflected back onto our own sense of identity and purpose. My friend, Darrell Johnson, pastor of Glendale Presbyterian Church, California, explains it this way:

> Every image we create distorts God in some way, either ignoring something that is true of God or adding something that is not true of God. What's the big deal? The big deal is that we become like that which we worship. It's a law of nature. We become like that to which we give ultimate allegiance. The dimensions and qualities of our lives are directly proportional to how well we understand the Maker. To have a misunderstanding of the Maker is to have a misunderstanding of who we are. . . .
>
> In our pain, it is so easy to project another image of God and go astray. We end up with a false image of God and a false image of ourselves.[3]

Jesus refers to this dynamic in the Parable of the Talents (Matt. 25:14-30). The one-talent servant feared the master and hid his talent. His unhealthy fear led to an unfruitful life and a broken relationship. When we have an unhealthy fear of God, there is no relationship of love. The best we can hope for is an association based on obligation. This servant expressed no personal loyalty to the Master. He wanted to fulfill his duty and be done with it. This servant thinks in terms of getting by with the minimum. This mentality of "covering ourselves," so that we won't get into trouble, reveals again that this relationship is viewed solely in terms of duty and obligation.

We are left in this quandary: How are we to know God

truly, perceiving God's nature and work as accurately as possible in this life? How do we overcome the limitations of human reasoning and experience?

We have hope because God has revealed the truth about Himself in the Bible. This truth taps springs of hope and joy, springs that can refresh aching souls, renew flagging wills, and reawaken the desire to be what the Lord who loves us created us to be.

The Journey into a Healthy View of God

The "fear of the Lord" which Proverbs proclaims as the beginning of wisdom is rooted in a love and acceptance that are far deeper than any we have ever known before. God does not want us to be afraid of Him, as if He were an antagonistic policeman watching for the least mistake. God is not interested in legalism for the sake of keeping score in a game that we are bound to lose. God is interested in our wholeness, our restoration, for the sake of joy and health and fullness of life!

My own definition of the healthy fear of God is: *The fear of the Lord is that deep and abiding sense of appreciation and love for God which inspires me to live in a manner that reflects my devotion and respect for God and God's will.* Because of the depth of His love and sacrifice for me, I do not want to offend God or cause any reason for others to condemn His name. The fear of the Lord is the beginning of wisdom because it is the smartest way to live!

In order to break loose from the unhealthy fear of God, we can take at least two specific steps. The first is receiving a true understanding of God's person and work from God's Word. The truth will set us free from our unbiblical ideas about God. The starting place for our meditation is to look at the life of Jesus Christ. The Old Testament has an important place which I will describe in a moment, but Jesus lived so that we could most clearly see what God is like. Humans have always had a difficult time trying to perceive God accurately. As John 1:18 says, "No one has ever seen God. It is God the only Son, who is close to the Father's heart, who has made Him known" (NRSVB). When we want to see what God is like, we are instructed to look at Jesus. This same message is given to Philip and the other disciples, "Anyone who has seen Me has seen the Father. How can you say, 'Show us the Father'? Don't you believe that I am in the Father and that the Father is in Me?" (John 14:9-10)

As we study the life of Jesus, we see the mix of majesty in stilling the storm and of humility in taking a child on His lap. We see His stern judgment against those who play intellectual games with religious topics and His infinite patience with those who are trying—trying so hard—to understand. Above all, we see those who knew Him best loving Him more and more and more as they drew closer to Him. Meditation on the life and teaching of Jesus fills our minds with new images of One we can trust, One who is able to understand our pain, and One who is ready to hear our cry, "Lord, we believe; help our unbelief."

The second step to breaking free from unhealthy fear is to release our pain to God. Experiences of abuse and disappointment leave deep marks on our souls. They do not wear off with time. They usually penetrate more deeply if left unattended. The process of release takes as many forms as there are people, but it will often include several basic elements. The first is the touch of hope that stirs courage within the soul to face up to the pain. Pray for God to touch you, or one you are concerned about. The Spirit's timing is perfect.

When this courage awakens, do not postpone taking the next step of bringing the pain to the light. This usually involves some type of conversation with a pastor, counselor, spiritual director, or mature friend in Christ. It can also happen through writing a letter to God, or writing in a journal. The full impact of the release is best realized, however, when someone else hears your story and pronounces you free in the name of Jesus Christ. That person's witness to your pain and to God's faithfulness provides a concrete step forward. It marks the occasion so that you have a checkpoint for reference when the inevitable doubts and fears come knocking again on your door. You can look them straight in the eye and say, "Remember when I gave all that stuff to Jesus? I do not have it any longer! You'll have to see Him about it now. I am free!"

The interaction of new information about God, gleaned from meditation on God's Word, along with experiences of releasing painful memories to God combine to generate spiritual health and vitality. Both dimensions are necessary to touch our hearts and minds with the grace of God.

Living with the Fear That Makes Us Unafraid

The fear of God frees us from all other fears. I once heard a benediction which always generates appreciative comments from people:

> May you love God so much
>   that you will love nothing else too much;
> May you fear God enough
>   that you will fear nothing else at all.[4]

When we are tempted to be afraid, we stop and ask ourselves, "Afraid of what? What is the worst that can happen here?" Fears that are grabbed by the scruff of the neck and made to give an account are like bullies that back off when they are challenged by a confident authority.

Jesus gave this advice to His disciples as a reality check. "Do not fear those who kill the body but cannot kill the soul; rather fear Him who can destroy both soul and body in hell" (Matt. 10:28, NRSVB). Small comfort, you say, considering the blunt language of destroying the body and soul? Then continue to read as Jesus describes the orientation of the One "who can destroy both soul and body in hell." "Are not two sparrows sold for a penny? Yet not one of them will fall to the ground apart from the will of your Father. And even the very hairs of your head are numbered. So do not be afraid; you are of more value than many sparrows" (vv. 29-31). The One who could ultimately destroy us is the One who intimately knows us. He completely cares for us. This truth unmasks the lies and distortions of fear, sending the bullies on their way.

Our fear in life is inversely proportional to our experience of God's presence. As we cultivate an evermore accurate concept of God through the study of His written Word, we shine the bright light of truth against the frightening shadows cast by the world, the flesh, and the devil. As our vital experience of the Living Word, Jesus Christ, grows, His presence brightens our lives, driving out the darkness. Yes, there will be concern and moments of trepidation, but they will not freeze us into inaction.

The fear of the Lord becomes the guiding principle, shaping our perspective and our daily decisions. Consider again my suggested definition: *The fear of the Lord is that deep and abiding sense of appreciation and love for God which inspires me to live in a manner that reflects my devotion and respect for God and God's will.* As our appreciation for God grows, so does our commitment to honor the name of the Lord in every dimension. This is the essence of the petition in the Lord's Prayer, "Our Father, which art in heaven, *hallowed be Thy name.*" Practical actions flow from our new understanding. We enjoy a deepening fellowship with God, a broadening service in the power of God, and a growing confidence in the resources of God.

Fearful ideas of God are the product of minds held captive to lies. In Jesus Christ, we are given the key to release us from bondage. He has given us the truth that takes every thought captive to obey Christ (see 2 Cor. 10:5). Like Gideon, our freedom begins with tearing down the idols in our own lives and allowing God to be God. Take the hammer and be strong!

Investing in Your "R & D"
Questions for Reflection and Discussion

1. Reflect on the "diagnostic questions" that the author suggests can help you know if you have some fear-formed idols.
   a. "What are the first thoughts that come to mind when I think of the Lord? Do these thoughts draw me closer to God and encourage me as a person? Or do I feel resistant to God and uncomfortable at the thought of drawing closer?"
   b. "What characteristics of God are most important to me? Where did I develop my concept of these characteristics? From the Bible or from my experience?"
   c. "How do I respond when I hear teaching on the grace and goodness of God? Do I celebrate God, or find myself waging an inner battle with resentment toward God?"
2. Which perception of God do you find most common in your relationships and conversations with others?
   a. Deal-Maker
   b. The Angry One
   c. The Busy One
   d. The Demanding One

3. What "fear-formed idol" of God are you most tempted to create?

4. Do you agree with Tozer's assertion that, *"We tend by a secret law of the soul to move toward our mental image of God"*? What evidence have you seen that supports your opinion?

5. What other types of "idols" do you encounter from listening to people or observing their lives?

People think God is like us!

6. Which do you think has had the most influence on people's negative perceptions of God: limited education or painful experience? Why? Give specific examples if you can.

If they knew they would understand

7. What aspect of God do you most desire to experience? Can you think of any Gospel stories where this is displayed in Jesus?

His ~~affec~~ affirmation of my worship

8. Respond to the author's suggested definition of the fear of the Lord: *The fear of the Lord is that deep and abiding sense of appreciation and love for God which inspires me to live in a manner that reflects my devotion and respect for God and God's will.*

a. What do you find helpful about this definition?

b. What is your own definition?

Respect his authority
+ power + position

but *love* Him

obey Him

trust Him

Chapter Six

Immortal Lessons from Our Mortality

Sarah Winchester's husband had accumulated a vast fortune by manufacturing and selling rifles. After he died of influenza in 1918, she moved to San Jose, California. In her grief, Sarah pursued her interest in spiritism. When she sought out a medium to contact her dead husband, the medium told her, "As long as you keep building your home, you will never face death."

Sarah believed the spiritist. She purchased an unfinished seventeen-room mansion and started building. The project continued until she died thirty-eight years later at the age of eighty-five. It cost 5 million dollars at a time when workmen earned fifty cents a day. The mansion had grown to 150 rooms, 13 bathrooms, 2,000 doors, 47 fireplaces, and 10,000 windows. It contained stairways that led nowhere and doors that opened into walls. When construction stopped at her death, enough materials remained to have continued building for another eighty years![1]

The writer of Hebrews speaks of "those who through fear of death were subject to lifelong bondage" (see Heb. 2:15). Today, the Winchester House stands as more than a tourist attraction. It is a silent witness to the dread of death that holds millions of people in bondage. While Sarah Winchester may be an extreme example of the fear of death, she has many comrades who construct complicated systems to avoid facing the reality of our human condition.

Our preoccupation with health and fitness, combined with our intense resistance to death, makes us especially vulnerable to the fear of the one certainty of life: death. Many have observed that death is the "new obscenity." We are unwilling to talk about it, to accept it, and to acknowledge that it is a natural part of life. Our emphasis on health is admirable. Problems rise, however, when our preoccupation blinds us to the reality that we are "of dust and to dust we will return" (Gen. 3:19).

As difficult as it seems, we will do better if we keep the reality of our mortality before us than if we deny it. Philip, King of Macedonia, a province of ancient Greece, charged a slave to remind him every morning: "Philip, remember that you must die."[2] Few of us can imagine dealing with such a stark pronouncement daily. It touches the central nerve of fear in our lives. I cannot probe this area without sending shooting pain through most, if not all, who read this. As I wrote the initial draft of this chapter, a beautiful young wife and mother of three in our congregation succumbed after a six-year ordeal with cancer. I do not write these thoughts from an ivory tower, but from the bedsides and hospital rooms of those who are facing these issues right now.

We all know people, and may be among them ourselves, who have lost a loved one, who are living with chronic pain, or have been informed that they are HIV positive. No one can fully understand the terror and dread which threaten to suffocate us as we confront these circumstances. But there is relief in Jesus Christ. The way to it, however, requires "gritting our teeth" through the pain in order to come out on the other side.

The fear in sickness, aging, and death is comprised of at least four basic elements:

1. fear of pain;
2. fear that we will lose control and suffer indignity;
3. fear that we will be abandoned by others;
4. and fear that we will be cut off from the peace, presence, and care of God.

These fears revolve around a number of losses: our loss of comfort, loss of freedom, loss of ability, loss of vitality, and above all, our loss of connection with others and our Lord. These fears are common to humankind. The testimony of Scripture is that these feelings do arise within "real believers." They come to all of us. But these fears do not reflect the full truth about God's relationship with us. Nor do they limit our response options. The truth will involve mysteries we cannot comprehend, but our faith can be strengthened in the midst of these circumstances as the Lord leads us through them.

There are many profound lessons that we seem to learn only when we are on our backs, looking up. They are lessons from the classroom of pain, taught by the instructor, Suffering. *Where fear makes human suffering a barrier to the fullness of life, faith can make it a bridge to the presence, peace, and power of God.* If we can begin to understand some of these lessons in times of health, we can be better prepared to cope with the inevitable challenges of our mortality.

The Lesson of Mystery

Our starting point is one of humility in the face of a mystery we can never fully comprehend. Suffering is like beauty: we can say much about it, but we can never explain it. Above all, we cannot justify it. The only person who can justify the role of suffering is the sufferer, and then she can only justify it for herself. Suffering faces us with a mystery we will never comprehend in this life.

But the very acknowledgment of mystery provides a large measure of comfort. Many years ago I heard Corrie Ten Boom, author of *The Hiding Place,* tell of her family's costly commitment to hide Jews fleeing from Nazi persecution at the outbreak of World War II. She told of the time when, as a young girl, she asked her father why God allowed all the suffering and sadness they were seeing.

Her father said, "Corrie, before I answer your question, would you go over and pick up my satchel and bring it here?" He was a watch repairman, and his satchel of tools and watch parts was very heavy. Corrie went over and tried to pick it up.

She couldn't even budge it. She wanted to please her father, so she tried it again and again. But it just wouldn't move.

She went to her father and said, "Father, I'm sorry, but your satchel is too heavy for me to carry." Her father then looked at her and said, "Corrie, the answer to the question you are asking me is like that satchel. It is too heavy for you to carry at this time. Let me carry it until you are older."

We are often unable to carry the answers to the questions we ask of God. Like Corrie, we learn to accept the necessity of mystery and to trust the One who can carry the solutions for us.

The experience of the Apostle Paul described in 2 Corinthians 12 illustrates one who has come to terms with the mystery of his suffering. Paul first tells of his experience of the glory of paradise. "I know a man in Christ who fourteen years ago was caught up to the third heaven—whether it was in the body or out of the body I do not know—God knows. And I know that this man—whether in the body or apart from the body I do not know—God knows—was caught up to the third heaven. . . . He heard inexpressible things, that man is not permitted to tell" (2 Cor. 12:2-4). Paul highlights the side of mystery we so often fail to acknowledge: if there is a mystery to suffering, there is also the mystery of goodness and blessing.

Why are we privileged to enjoy so many good things? Why does food taste good? Why is water so refreshing? Why is procreation in the context of sexual pleasure? Why are there animals that can serve as our companions and protectors? Why? If we seek an explanation for suffering, wisdom, and fairness suggest we also seek an explanation for life's blessings.

But Paul's experience resulted in something we may never have expected: the grief of a satanic thorn. "To keep me from becoming too conceited because of these surpassingly great revelations, there was given me a thorn in my flesh, a messenger of Satan, to torment me" (12:7). Paul does not define his thorn. This was a wise decision. He understood the tendency of human beings to pass judgment on another's interpretations of his situation. In the sanctuary of his own soul-communion with the Lord, he had come to terms with his condition. His interpretation of suffering as a messenger of Satan who serves God's purposes challenges us to carefully consider our particular situations. Prayerful dialogue with God can bring a sense of perspective and understanding impossible for human logic.

Nevertheless, we cannot duck the tough questions about the hiddenness of God and His purpose in times of suffering and death. We dare not join with the prophets of Judah who would say, " 'Peace, peace' . . . when there is no peace" (Jer. 6:14). Jeremiah describes these prophets as ones who "dress the wound of [God's] people as though it were not serious" (v. 14). Offering easy answers to life's deepest pain is like putting a dirty bandage on a compound fracture. Instead, we stand in trusting humility before the Almighty. By God's grace, we may receive some sense of His purpose. But more than that, we will discover the strength of His presence which can be even more vivid in our weakness.

The Lesson of Our Mortality

Having humbled ourselves before the Lord, we now look carefully at our existence and our expectations for life. At the very heart of this subject is the fact of our humanity, and more specifically, our mortality. In the Garden we suffered a mortal wound. Death in its many manifestations permeated the creation. But God did not leave us without hope. In Jesus Christ, we received resurrection hope. Like Jesus, we pass to that new life through the doorway of the grave. The grave is not our only enemy. The forces of death permeate every dimension of life. Death has intertwined itself in the created order in the forces of chaos and decay, in our relationships so often shaken by distrust and division, and in our very selves through intellectual, moral, and emotional conflict.

The physical reality of illness, aging, and dying are the most vivid reminders that we are "dusty people." We do not, however, want to be reminded of this fact. The psalmist wrote, "for He knows how we are formed, He remembers that we are dust" (Ps. 103:14). Do we remember? If so, this fact is frequently eclipsed by other claims and promises. Our expectations are fed and inflated daily by the visions of beauty and physical vitality captured on film and dancing over the air-waves. We go after dust with the vacuum cleaner of denial, and then wonder why we have such a hard time with life's hard knocks.

We presume that sickness is abnormal, something we should never have to cope with. Our idealistic, distorted, irrational thinking makes us vulnerable to greater psychological complications from sickness than the physiological problems of the disease. Sickness is part of being human, though it is a consequence of the Fall. We do well to heed the instruction of James 4:13-16:

> Now listen, you who say, "Today or tomorrow we will go to this or that city, spend a year there, carry on business and make money." Why, you do not even know what will happen tomorrow. What is your life? You are a mist that appears for a little while and then vanishes. Instead, you ought to say, "If the Lord will, we will live and we shall do this or that." As it is, you boast and brag. All such boasting is evil.

We do not think like James because we have found many ways to shield ourselves from the threats of life. Consider how our expectations concerning illness have changed dramatically since the discovery of penicillin. This can be seen in the way in which the role of doctors has changed. Before antibiotics, a doctor's task was often that of comfort and relief for a person during the process of dying. Such is no longer the case. The progress of medical science has brought us to the point where the doctors and medical staff are the cavalry, and death is the enemy to whom we refuse to surrender. We are beginning to demand cures as if they were among our inalienable rights, instead of receiving them as gifts.

I received a special lesson on mortality on a beautiful summer day. My teenage son, Matthew, and I were climbing the backside of Half Dome in Yosemite National Park, California. It is an 8.2 mile trail hike one way, with a vertical rise of 4,800 feet. After over four and a half hours of climbing, we were on the steep granite side of the Dome, walking with the help of steel cables anchored to the steep rock surface. Within sight of our goal, I nearly blacked out. We were just 400 feet from the summit, but I honestly did not think I could make it to the top. Jim and his son, Jared, were climbing with us. Jim came to my rescue, standing with me, giving me some of his water and candy for a boost of energy. After a frightening fifteen or twenty minutes, I began to feel strength trickling back. Another twenty minutes, and I began to complete the slow ascent to the summit—where the view was incredible—and even sweeter for the scare!

I learned a clear lesson about mortality: my willpower could not overcome my physical limitations. My failure to carry enough water and to eat more complex carbohydrates in preparation for the hike had left me vulnerable to the demands of that rigorous climb. But I don't want you to misunderstand the point. I was frightened as I sat on the barren rock, over eight miles from my car. I had no idea how we would get off the Dome without help, and I did not want the attention of any rescue efforts! We dare not devalue the agony by somehow "cashing in" on the pain as we draw lessons from it. It is simplistic, if not cruel and inhumane, to say that the purpose of sickness or suffering is to make us appreciate health. That is like banging cymbals over a person's head to make them appreciate silence! Still, we will find strength to endure as we acknowledge that we are dust and develop our expectations accordingly.

The Lesson of Honesty

When we begin with the reality of a God whose ways we will never fully understand, and with our dusty humanity, many of our pretensions are stripped away. We can begin to learn the lesson of honesty. I once called a woman who, with her husband, had undergone extensive procedures for infertility. I heard that the procedures were not successful, so I called to check in with her.

After our conversation, she said, "Thanks so much for calling to ask how I'm doing. Fewer people are asking as time goes on."

"I realize that I find it difficult to bring up the subject," I confessed. "I guess we don't want to remind you of the pain."

"But when you ask me, I don't feel so invisible," she said. What a powerful observation! She was commenting on the dynamics of denial and avoidance that swirl around the issues of illness, aging, and death.

We fear facing the truth about ourselves and our circumstances. Part of the burden of illness or aging is the fear of sharing honestly how we feel as we struggle through the process. When we feel most vulnerable, we are tempted to defend ourselves against exposure. We don't want people to judge us as weak, or reject us as whiners. So we suffer silently, denying ourselves the support of others who face what we face.

Honesty unites us with others, especially the honesty of admitting our needs. In a relationship of love and trust, we connect most strongly at our weakest points. Being honest, however, carries its own set of fears: fear of appearing weak, fear of being rejected, fear of finding the truth much, much harder to bear. Still, the words of Jesus apply to life as well as to theology: "You will know the truth, and the truth will set you free" (John 8:32).

The Lesson of Grace (2 Cor. 12:9-11)

Grace is not overcome by age, disease, or even by death. Grace is the death-defeater. Grace enables us to see in the mystery of life, not the threat of antagonistic forces, but the immense wisdom and love of the Lord God who understands how we are made. It enables us to face our mortality with the hope of immortality, to accept the limitations of our humanity, and to be honest in the light of integrity and vulnerability.

"My grace is sufficient for you, for My power is made perfect in weakness," says the Lord. How so? It is a basic law of the physical universe that two objects cannot occupy the same space. One displaces the other. Two cars cannot occupy the same traffic lane, as we have seen with tragic results. Likewise, two powers cannot occupy the same "spiritual space." One displaces the other. When we are strong in ourselves—and there are times when such is appropriate—we are not relying on the exceptional intervention of God. But when we find ourselves empty, confronted with circumstances which exhaust our own resources, then we tap the living waters of the Lord.

The essence of grace is the surpassing generosity of God which is showered upon us in spite of our unworthiness. This grace is revealed primarily in Jesus Christ, who took our place in suffering the justice of God so that we could be pardoned from the consequences of our disobedience. I once explained it this way to a real estate agent: Imagine that you have just sold an immense parcel of land. The new owner comes back to you and sues you because the land is contaminated with toxic waste. The judge rules that you are liable for damages running into the tens of millions of dollars. But then something strange happens. The judge steps down from the bench and steps into your place.

"I have arranged to have you pardoned. I will pay all damages and arrange for the entire clean-up of the property. Now, go home. You are free."

We can never chart the dimensions of grace. We will always run out of paper! The grace of God touches not only matters of life and death, but matters of living and dying. God's gift of grace is for each moment of every day. What did this mean for the Apostle Paul? It meant strength to continue his ministry in spite of his struggles. An example of this was at Galatia. He preached to the Galatians during a time of illness (was this a manifestation of the thorn?) and found the people welcomed him as if he were an angel (Gal. 4:14). His weakness evoked the strength of caring in the community.

The lessons we have explored thus far lay the foundation for our practical response in dealing with the specific situation that is arousing fear within us. They will help us move forward in acceptance and adjustment to our life circumstance.

The Lessons of Acceptance and Adjustment

"All the more gladly I will boast about my weaknesses, so that Christ's power may rest on me. That is why, for Christ's sake, I delight in weaknesses, in insults, in hardships, in persecutions, in difficulties. For when I am weak, then I am strong" (2 Cor. 12:9-10).

A couple who have helped me understand what this looks like are Bob and Marilynn Krum, members of our congregation.³ At midlife, Bob was diagnosed with multiple sclerosis (MS), a condition in which scar tissue gradually replaces the myelin sheath on the spinal column and obstructs the nerve impulses. After thirty years of deterioration, Bob eventually needed a cane to walk with, became confined to a wheelchair, and then became quadriplegic.

Bob was not sure how he would adjust to the ever-increasing limitations this disease imposed on him. He had an example that caused him much concern. When his father had been confronted in his early fifties with an undiagnosed illness, he had taken his own life. Would Bob succumb to the pressure of despair?

As Bob told me, the Lord had been preparing him for a long time.

"In 1975," said Bob, "I had an experience with the Living God. During that experience, I read Isaiah 48:10-11, where the Lord said, 'Behold, I have refined you, though not as silver; I have tested you in the furnace of affliction. For My own sake, for My own sake, I do this.' After that experience, my life was transformed. I began each day asking God, 'I need Your strength, Your power, Your *Dunamis,* for that day.'"

At that time, Bob knew he had MS, but he had no idea how bad it would become. As they walked this journey of chronic illness, Bob and Marilynn continually turned to their faith. They came to understand that, as Bob frequently says, "Real life is seen from the perspective of eternity."

While most of us are tempted to get lost in the struggle with illness itself, Bob and Marilynn turned to learning how to live a full life in the light of limitations. A significant step in this direction came when group of churches in Fresno purchased a voice-activated computer system linked to a high-tech telephone system. From his bedroom, Bob was able to handle telephone referrals for a local Christian ministry of compassion, Evangelicals for Social Action/LOVE, INC. (The 'INC' stands for "*I*n the *N*ame of Christ.") As he located volunteers from his church to help those in need, they usually had no idea that they were speaking to a quadriplegic confined to bed.

The voice-activated computer has opened other doors as well. Bob and Marilynn have founded an organization called Mainstream Solution Resources, providing information, training, and funding for handicapped individuals, especially with the aid of computer technology.

Bob and Marilynn are credible witnesses to the power of God to overcome the fear of illness. They are very honest about their struggles. "We aren't included in many things, even at church," Bob said, "because it is so hard to get me moved around."

"And we do struggle with fear about the future. We are not sure how this disease will progress," says Marilynn.

"But I have been born to a living hope," says Bob, with a tear streaming down his cheek. "When you've been where I've been, there isn't much more to fear."

A living hope—in the midst of a situation where most of us are tempted to despair. The Krums, like the Apostle Paul, have learned that the power of God is sufficient in our weakness. Their ministry has literally touched lives around the world through a video produced by World Vision. They have been used by God to reach the handicapped in ways they have never been reached before. Where does the strength come from to handle this type of suffering? It comes from an experience with the Living God.

The lessons of acceptance and adjustment are the most difficult because they mean laying down our expectations, our dreams, our deepest hopes and desires. It's no accident that acceptance comes near the end of a process. Some become discouraged because they think we must begin with this step. That's just not realistic. To require acceptance from the beginning is like demanding that a preschooler write essays. They lack the physical capabilities as well as the intellectual development for such a task. Likewise, our ability to process the trials of life means that we must unlearn many false assumptions, shed many unrealistic expectations, and delve deeply into our souls.

Facing the Ultimate Enemy

No matter how much we prepare, we cannot escape the pain of parting from loved ones and life itself. Biblically speaking, death continues to be an enemy. In 1 Corinthians 15:25-26 we read, "For He [Jesus Christ] must reign until He has put all His enemies under His feet. The last enemy to be destroyed is death." We cannot theologize ourselves into numbness when we face our own struggle or that even more painful struggle of standing at the bedside of ones we love. The loss is real, and the separation can result in a tearing that will leave a scar.

There are several specific principles which can help us face death with spiritual courage. First is the fact that death releases us from the bondage of sin and its consequences. One of the ironies of life is that freedom from the effects of mortality is found only through succumbing to it. In eternal life, the Lord "will wipe every tear from their eyes. There will be no more death or mourning or crying or pain, for the old order of things has passed away" (Rev. 21:4). We will finally put off the old nature with its passions and weakness. We will be able to link godly desires with obedient responses. The battle will be over!

Second, that the fear of death makes death all the more difficult. Jeremy Taylor, in his classic treatise, *The Rule and Exercises of Holy Living and the Rule and Exercises of Holy Dying*, gives wise counsel concerning the fear of death. Taylor writes,

> ... fear gives to death wings, and spurs and darts. Death hastens to a fearful man ... If thou wilt be fearless of death ... be once persuaded to believe that there is a condition of living better than this; that there are creatures more noble than we; that above there is a country better than ours ..."[4]

We all can relate to the situation of a child receiving a shot of medicine with a needle. Her screaming and squirming can make the entire process much more of an ordeal than it needs to be. Perhaps it's too much to expect passive acceptance, but a courageous effort makes it easier for all involved.

Taylor reminds us that death is not merely an intrusion into life. Rather, he calls it "the harbor," the destination of this earthly voyage. He writes:

God having in this world placed us in a sea, and troubled the sea with a continual storm, hath appointed the church for a ship, and religion to be the stern; but there is no haven nor port but death. Death is that harbour whither God hath designed every one, that there he may find rest from the troubles of the world.

Either therefore let us be willing to die when God calls, or let us never more complain of the calamities of our life which we feel so sharp and numerous. And when God sends His angel to us with the scroll of death, let us look on it as an act of mercy, to prevent many sins and many calamities of a longer life, and lay our heads down softly, and go to sleep without wrangling like babies and froward children. For a man at least gets this by death, that his calamities are not immortal.[5]

This is the stern advice of the Puritan era which is more straightforward than we are accustomed to. We may long for a bit more empathy, for the acknowledgment of genuine pain and difficult questions which are not silenced in our souls by theological truth. Nevertheless, his principles shore up a flagging soul.

Sir Arthur John Gossip was a preacher and professor of practical theology and Christian ethics at Glasgow University, Scotland. He preached one of the finest sermons in the history of Christian preaching immediately after the sudden death of his young wife. His sermon, entitled, "But When Life Tumbles in, What Then?" reveals a profound struggle between faith and grief, the questions of the mind and the beliefs of the heart. As he wrestles to a glorious victory, he calls us to look beyond our own loneliness to the joy our loved ones have gained. Speaking of his wife's entrance into heaven he writes,

I love to picture it. How, shyly, amazed, half protesting, she who never thought of self was led into the splendor of her glory. . . . To us it will be long and lonesome: but they won't even have looked round them before we burst in. In any case, are we to let our dearest be wrenched out of our hands by force? Or, seeing that it has to be, will we not give them willingly and proudly, looking God in the eyes, and telling Him that we prefer our loneliness rather than that they should miss one tittle of their rights.[6]

Viewing death from the perspective of eternity transforms it from the specter which has stripped us of all joy. We see the glory of God's grace in Christ which gives a joy nothing can take from us. This is when we begin to understand Paul's bold assertion, " 'Death has been swallowed up in victory. Where, O death, is your victory? Where, O death, is your sting?' The sting of death is sin, and the power of sin is the law. But thanks be to God! He gives us the victory through our Lord Jesus Christ" (1 Cor. 15:54-56). Death does not have the last word.

Gossip concludes his message with a resounding note of confidence:

I don't think you need be afraid of life. Our hearts are very frail; and there are places where the road is very steep and very lonely. But we have a wonderful God. And as Paul puts it, what can separate us from His love? Not death, he says immediately, pushing that aside at once as the most obvious of all impossibilities.

No, not death. For standing in the roaring of the Jordan, cold to the heart with its dreadful chill, and very conscious of the terror of its rushing, I too, like Hopeful [in *Pilgrim's Progress*] can call back to you who one day in your turn will have to cross it, "Be of cheer, my brother, for I feel the bottom, and it is sound."[7]

Preparing Daily for Crisis

The time to purchase batteries is before the storm strikes. The time to practice free throws is before the championship basketball game. The time to study for the final exam is prior to the final minutes before the test. The best time to prepare for the challenges of aging, illness, and death is now.

This preparation involves every area of life. We want to lay God's Word up in our hearts. We want to cultivate our prayer conversation with the Lord, so that we know some of the deeper means of communion with Him. We want to cultivate our relationships through intentional caring and integrity so that we are free from regret and free to draw on the investment of love when we are in need. We want to be wise stewards of each day, not presuming on the future to make up for carelessness today. As Moses wrote, "Teach us to number our days aright, that we may gain a heart of wisdom" (Ps. 90:12).

The Lord is faithful, He will strengthen + protect you from the evil one   II Thess 3:3

II Tim 4:18 the Lord will rescue me from every evil attack + will bring me safely to His heavenly Kingdom. To Him be glory forever and ever Amen

Psalm 23:4 Even though I walk through the valley of the shadow of death I will fear no evil for you are with me. Your rod & your staff they comfort me.

Mother Theresa is beautiful

INVESTING IN YOUR "R & D"
QUESTIONS FOR REFLECTION AND DISCUSSION

1. What has been your experience with personal illness? How have you coped with it? *death in family Parents - sister*

2. What effect does the fact that the American culture glorifies youth have on our expectations concerning aging, illness, and death? What are some messages that people need to hear to counteract the unrealistic images of advertising and the media? *Sara 90 still gorgeous - beauty was character*

3. The older we get, the more apparent it becomes that we are "dusty people." Our bodies slow down, wear out, or just don't do what they used to do. What have you learned about acceptance and your own mortality from this process? *maturing - to the fullness God has for us*

4. The author suggests five lessons to be learned from mortality.
   a. Which lesson strikes you as most troubling and difficult to accept? Why? *Acceptance*
   b. Which lesson do you find most helpful? Why? *Grace - mercy*
   c. What other lessons can you draw from your own thinking and experience? *Appreciation of life around me - no taking for granted*

5. Death is difficult for many to discuss. The following questions may be too sensitive for you to discuss with others, but reflect carefully on them. There may a time you would be able to discuss them with significant people in your life.
   a. If you were diagnosed with a terminal medical condition, would you want to be told right away? *yes*
   b. How would you want to be told? *husband*
   c. What support system do you now have, or would you need to have, to cope with such a situation? *already have wonderful family + friends*

6. Do you have the courage to face death if it should come knocking today? What do you most fear about death? *how? when? No - Corrie Ten Boom story*

7. What specific steps of "daily preparation" would you like to begin to take to equip yourself and your loved ones to handle the issues raised in this chapter? *TRUST The steps of a righteous woman are ordered by the Lord*

Chapter Seven

Seeds of Hope
for Those Who Follow

One fear that persists across the span of time is the fear of what will happen to the next generation. As our first parents were expelled from the Garden, they heard the pronouncement of this terrible curse: "In sorrow thou shalt bring forth children" (Gen. 3:16, KJV). Experience has shown us that the sorrow and struggle related to children is not limited to the pain of childbirth. We might paraphrase the verse to say, "In sorrow shall you bring up children." It is not sorrow because of our children themselves, as if they caused it. It is sorrow in realizing what they have to face in their lives. The call of a parent does not end with the painful labor of birth; that's just the beginning. Fathers and mothers often experience the painful labor of birthing the character and skills within their children which prepare them for life outside the Garden, where we all live.

Life outside the garden is looking especially bleak these days. Perhaps it is a liability of aging, but maturing adults most often express weariness and fear, rather than excitement and hope, at the problems facing the next generation. What may be more unsettling at the present time is that the members of the rising generation themselves realize that they are looking at an uninviting landscape for the future.

In their book, *13th Generation: Abort, Retry, Ignore, Fail?*

Neil Howe and Bill Strauss explore the nature of America's thirteenth generation born between 1961–1981. They begin with this scenario:

> Imagine coming to a beach at the end of a long summer of wild goings-on. The beach crowd is exhausted, the sand shopworn, hot, and full of debris — no place for walking barefoot. You step on a bottle, and some cop yells at you for littering. The sun is directly overhead and leaves no patch of shade that hasn't already been taken. You feel the glare beating down on a barren landscape devoid of secrets or innocence. You look around at the disapproving faces and can't help but sense, somehow, that the entire universe is gearing up to punish you.[1]

Not a welcoming picture. This uninviting perception of the present and the future not only quenches the optimism of the "American Dream," but stirs the deepening cynicism and pessimism that are the stuff of nightmares. Our attempts to paint bright pictures for coming generations are like spraying perfume on a skunk: we may momentarily cover the odor, but we don't get to the heart of the problem. If we are to plant seeds of hope for those who will follow, we must first understand the climate and conditions in which they will be living.

A Generation at Risk

Statistics carry a bad rap for being cold and impersonal. But the following compilation of numbers contains many faces I have seen, many people I have hugged. How 'bout you?

> Every day, over 2,500 American children witness the divorce or separation of their parents. Every day, 90 kids are taken from their parents' custody and committed to foster homes.
> Every day, 13 Americans age 15 to 24 commit suicide, and another 16 are murdered. Every day, the typical 14-year-old watches 3 hours of TV and does 1 hour

of homework. Every day, over 2,200 kids drop out of school. Every day, 3,610 teenagers are assaulted, 630 are robbed, and 80 are raped.

Every day, over 100,000 high school students bring guns to school. Every day, 500 adolescents begin using illegal drugs and 1,000 begin drinking alcohol. Every day, 1,000 unwed teenage girls become mothers.[2]

As we shake our heads and click our tongues, the point is not that this is a "bad generation." The point is that their situation is bad. This brief study does not permit an in-depth exploration of the complex dynamics behind these terrifying social trends. We need to have some idea, however, of the reasons why one of the most prosperous countries in the world is producing a spiritually bankrupt society. While there's no easy explanation, Howe and Strauss present the outlines of the formula:

> What went wrong, and why? It's a simple formula, really. Take a generation of kids, give them crumbly families that don't allow them much time to learn skills that aren't immediately useful; give them inferior schooling to tarnish their reputation for competence; surround them with media that teach them to distrust any institutional avenue to career success. Then, when they're all ready to enter the adult labor force, push every policy lever conceivable—tax codes, entitlements, public debt, unfunded liabilities, labor laws, hiring practices—to tilt the economic playing field away from the young and toward the old.[3]

For some, the pressure can be too much. Kurt Cobain, age twenty-seven, soared to musical stardom with a message of intense disillusionment. His Seattle music group, "Nirvana," helped establish "grunge rock music." He had become the representative of the fatalistic outlook of present-day youth who are looking at a world shaken by the crumbling of the family structure and the lowering of their job and financial prospects, accompanied by the dramatic rise of violence and drug abuse. According to news reports, Cobain's next album was going to be, "I Hate My Life, I Want to Die." But we will never know for sure, since on April 8, 1994, Kurt put a gun to his head and fulfilled his wish.

I have heard Kurt's exact words spoken by teenagers. At a time when many of us would like to believe that the teenage years should be the "happy days" of life, the fact is that they are riddled with an unhappiness that can lead to devastating consequences.

I was with John Perkins, who founded Mendenhall Ministries and Voice of Calvary in Mississippi, and over the last ten years has established Harambee Ministry in Pasadena. He was asked to address the cause of the Los Angeles riots in April 1992, following the announcement of the verdict in the Rodney King case. John believes that the fundamental spark which ignited the riots is the fact that there is no family structure in the ghetto, so that the children are running their neighborhoods. Perkins went on to note that there have been other times in history when the family has been threatened, resulting in widows and orphans. In those times, however, the greater community was there to support and guide those without support from their immediate family. The biblical story of Ruth and Naomi provides a vivid example, with Boaz serving as the kinsman-redeemer for the widowed Ruth. The present-day ghetto, says Perkins, has no such community. In this tragic circumstance, Perkins calls on the church to support the indigenous leadership of the communities of the city in order to redevelop community and family life. "If we do not take time for the children," says John Perkins, "the children will be forced to take things into their own desperate hands."

His message addresses not only urban blacks, but all ethnic groups, all urban, all suburban, and all rural people. He is speaking not only of the children who are victims of urban blight, but also to those who are victims of the soul-blight of materialism and self-centeredness in the suburbs. *If we do not take time for the children, the children will be forced to take things into their own desperate hands.*

It is a fearful situation. But we are learning that fear is an alarm to awaken us to faith. We are also learning that perfect love casts out fear. What are the resources of love that can bring hope into these days?

A Generation Willing to Risk

The seeds of hope must be planted by us. This does not mean that we are taking the responsibility and the privilege of contribution from the rising generation. It means that we refuse to allow our own discouragement to cause us to disengage from active involvement with them. We must be a generation willing to risk for those who will follow us. *We will overcome our fear for the next generation as we better understand their perspective on life, encourage them with God's vision of hope, and empower them with the resources of God's Good News in Jesus Christ.* The message of God's Word and the experience of God's people equip us for such a time as this.

Imagine an era of political chaos. Civil war has been such a scourge that people of the same nation and tribal heritage have nearly exterminated each other. Social decency has ebbed to inhuman depths of degradation. Religious leaders are "on the take." No scruples dissuade them from financial fraud and sexual immorality. Sound like our generation? Try 3,200 years ago! While we are tempted to think our generation is the worst, teetering on the brink of disaster due to an apparent sociological death-wish, we can find many examples of similar circumstances in history.

The Book of Judges, which records events in Israel from approximately 1380 to 1050 B.C., describes a bleak period when "everyone did as he saw fit" (Jud. 17:6). It was the "do-your-own-thing" age of Israel—and people did! Women were treated with savage cruelty. The tribes of Israel, with their roots in a common family, were spilling each other's blood in civil strife. But in the midst of this darkness, the story of Hannah and the special birth of her son, Samuel, provides us with an insightful account of God sowing seeds of hope for a future generation.

Hannah was infertile. Her barrenness was viewed as a personal failure and a social embarrassment. For years and years, she had been mocked by her husband's other wife, Peninnah, who had children. Hannah's anguish could not be comforted, not even by her husband's special treatment and affection for her. In her sadness, she consistently worshiped the Lord, pouring out her heart in prayer. One year, when her family traveled to Shiloh, the place of the tabernacle, for sacrifice, she went before the Lord in prayer.

The Bible tells us:

> In bitterness of soul Hannah wept much and prayed to the Lord. And she made a vow, saying, "O Lord Almighty, if You will only look upon Your servant's misery and remember me, and not forget Your servant but give her a son, then I will give him to the Lord for all the days of his life, and no razor will ever be used on his head" (1 Sam. 1:10-11).

Her prayer was so intense and emotional that the high priest, Eli, thought she was drunk. He had rarely seen such earnest devotion in prayer. When she explained her request, Eli was moved to respond, "Go in peace, and may the God of Israel grant you what you have asked of Him" (v. 17). Hannah received the word in faith, and God fulfilled the desires of her heart for a child.

In this account, I find at least four seeds of hope which are sown in the midst of dark times. The first is the seed of affirming and valuing life.

The Seed of Affirming and Valuing Life

Our children will find the courage of faith for their days as they see clearly our affirmation of life, even when the sour odors of decay are in the air. For Hannah, this meant persisting in prayer for a child during evil, evil times. Little could she imagine that her son-to-be would become the shining light to lead Israel into a new era, as Samuel would one day anoint David as king. Her sight did not extend that far, but her faith did. She affirmed that her child could serve the Lord and make a difference.

We need to search for life-affirming actions in our day when juvenile homicides too often are the headlines. One of the most practical ways we can do this is by observing and listening carefully to the next generation. I have always been touched by a story told by the Rev. Bruce Thielemann about a time he was sitting in a restaurant. At the table next to him sat a mother, father, and their young son. The waitress came over to take their orders. Father ordered, Mother ordered.

"And what would you like?" the waitress asked the little boy.

"He will have a child-sized order of chicken à la king," his mother said.

"Would you like a hamburger?" the waitress said to the little boy.

"Yeah!"

"He would like a child-sized order of chicken à la king!" insisted his mother.

"What would you like on that hamburger? Catsup, mustard, onion?" the waitress asked the boy.

"I'd like catsup and mustard, but no onion . . ."

"Miss, I guess you didn't understand. He'd like a child-sized order of chicken à la king!" repeated the mother.

"Do you want a Coke to go with your hamburger and some french fries too?" asked the waitress.

"Yeah, I'd like that."

And with that the waitress turned and walked away.

Before the mother could say anything more in protest, the little boy looked up at his mother and said, "Gee, Mommy, she thinks I'm real."

When we pay attention to people, our love affirms them and makes them feel "real," like people who are worthwhile.[4]

When we pay attention, however, we risk discomfort as we allow their messages to reach our consciousness. We value a person by validating the fact that he or she has concerns and perspectives that are different from our own. This is tough, especially when values we treasure deeply are challenged consistently. It is also difficult to listen to intense expressions of anger and despair, or to be confronted with the paradoxical responses of apathy and malaise.

As we take the time to affirm the next generation, we need

to guard against responding in unconstructive ways. First, we may be tempted to take their comments personally and put up our defenses. This most often results because we want to escape the shadows of our own denied, unresolved issues. Our defensiveness will only serve to widen the gap, to strain the already stressed ties. A second unproductive response comes when we try to "help them" with the quick-fix solutions that deny their complex struggles. We know from our own experience that in tough times, we need less advice and more empathy. Hope often breaks through when we listen—directly and indirectly—to the expressions of others' fear and disillusionment, without blocking our awareness through our own fear. When we give focused attention, free from quick condemnations, comparisons, and judgmentalism, we communicate a valuing which opens doors of hope and cooperation.

Our most powerful affirmation is expressed in love which persists through the trials of alienation that so often characterize cross-generational relationships. I remember hearing widely respected author Joseph Bayly, who had also served as vice president of David C. Cook Publishing, speak at a summer conference in upstate New York. He told the story of teenage rebellion and heartbreak in his home.

The Baylys had experienced their share of tragedy. Of their three sons, one died at age five of leukemia, and another died at age eighteen from an accident. The third son, who later rebelled, had been three years old when his five-year-old brother died. He couldn't understand it. And when his other brother died, he was only ten.

As he reached late teenage years, he turned his back on his faith and on his parents. He began taking drugs and never showed any regard for his parents' values and rights. Finally Joe and his wife confronted him.

"If you can't live by the rules of our home, and can't respect our faith, you'll have to move out."

So, he moved out and went to live on campus in a house that was coed. He slept in a sleeping bag on the floor. The house was always a mess. It broke their hearts to see their son living that way, but it was his choice.

One night, after he'd been gone quite a few months, the

phone rang at 2 A.M. It was the police from a neighboring town. The officer said that they had picked up his son and wanted Joe to come at once to post bail.

Joe thought he'd heard the name of the town, but when he went to that police station, there was no record of his son being picked up. He thought of another town that sounded similar and went there. Again, nothing. He drove to five different police stations, searching for his son. None of them knew anything about his son.

By now, Joe figured it must have been a crank call, so he drove by the house his son was staying in. It was past 4 A.M. Joe walked into his son's room and saw him sleeping soundly. He didn't wake him up. He just went over, leaned down, kissed him, and left.

Soon, the Baylys noticed a change in their son. Within a year he had made a complete about-face and even felt called to begin seminary.

One day Joe asked his son, "When did this change all start?"

"Dad, it was that night (referring to the night of the crank call). When you came into the house, you thought I was sleeping, but I wasn't. When you didn't yell at me, or wake me, I was surprised. You kissed me. And I said, 'If my Dad loves me that much, I've *got* to change.' "

Bayly concluded, "Our love must last through whatever our children put us through."[5]

Love persevering in the face of defiance wins more battles than any human power or coercion we are tempted to leverage. Love, valuing and affirming life in concrete ways, moves us light years ahead on the journey of hope.

The Seed of Dedication to God

The second seed of hope planted by Hannah was that of deepening dedication to the Lord. This is seen most clearly in her prayer. We need to note, however, that she suffered for a number of years before she prayed the prayer of 1 Samuel 1. She was like many of us: we try to deal with our pain on our own before calling out earnestly to the Lord. We need not chastise ourselves for past resistance. But now is the time for us to turn to the Lord, and to teach our children.

Hannah's dependence on God is clear from her prayer and her decision to dedicate her child as a gift for God's service. Her promise that a razor would never touch her son's hair was a commitment for him to be a Nazirite. Numbers 6 describes a Nazirite as a person dedicated to God for a special purpose. For some, this was for a limited period of time. For others, such as Samson and Samuel and John the Baptist, it was for a lifetime.

Hannah's commitment was far more than a bargain with the Lord. To see her prayer in such self-centered terms is to degrade both Hannah and the Lord. Hannah was revealing the depths of her heart's devotion. She wanted to offer God the most precious sacrifice of all: the fruit of her own and her husband's lives, a child whom they could commit to God's service. Think more carefully about what she was offering. After the child was weaned, which we may suppose from Hebrew custom would have been around age two, she was willing to give her child up to the care of Eli the high priest, who lived in a different town (1 Sam. 1:22). Then, she would see him only once a year (v. 19). Her love for her child would grow stronger with each passing day, yet she would separate from him and yield him to God's service. She would not watch him grow day by day. She would not hear his laughter, answer his questions, nor dry his tears. Does that sound like a good bargain for Hannah? Does that sound like a selfish request? It sounds to me like a supreme sacrifice.

Hannah was blessed by God as He gave her other children, but we can never imagine that the others replaced Samuel. What we learn from Hannah, however, is a lesson that can help us all: the next generation does, in fact, belong to the Lord. They do not belong to us. We are to be stewards of them for God, but they are in God's ultimate care. I believe Hannah's deep understanding of this principle set her free from anxious control and possessiveness. If we can begin to live in this confidence, we can experience a genuine freedom from fear for those who follow us.

The Seed of Listening to God

Our dedication to God is nurtured by our relationship with God. This means that we learn to listen for and recognize God's voice and teach our children to as well. We read in 1 Samuel 3:1, "The boy Samuel ministered before the Lord under Eli. In those days the word of the Lord was rare; there were not many visions." These words describe a desperate time. The people of God live by the Word of God. The Word of God, given in Scripture and in the vital fellowship of prayer, sustains us. When the Word is rare, despair is rampant.

The rarity of revelation in these days was more than a comment on God's willingness or unwillingness to speak; it was an indictment of the people's inability to listen. This inability was the result of spiritual apathy and antipathy toward the Lord. Eli, the high priest, had not rebuked his sons for their wicked behavior in the tabernacle service. Their flagrant disobedience to God's commandments was characteristic of the rest of the people. They became spiritually hard of hearing because their hearts were hard toward God.

One night, the Lord broke the silence. Samuel was lying down in the tabernacle, near Eli, when he heard his name called. Samuel ran to Eli and said, "Here I am." But Eli said that he had not called Samuel and told him to go back and lie down. This happened two more times. Then Eli realized it must be the Lord calling Samuel. He told Samuel, "Go and lie down, and if He calls you, say, 'Speak, Lord, for Your servant is listening' " (1 Sam. 3:9). Samuel did this, and the Lord gave him a message of judgment against Eli and his house. Samuel was afraid to tell Eli the vision, but Eli coaxed it from him. Then we read this description of Samuel,

> The Lord was with Samuel as he grew up, and He let none of his words fall to the ground. And all Israel from Dan to Beersheba recognized that Samuel was attested as a prophet of the Lord. The Lord continued to appear at Shiloh and there He revealed himself to Samuel through His Word (vv. 19-21).

Why did God break the silence? Ultimately, that remains a mystery of the Almighty. I do not have an exegetical basis for the following idea, but my personal opinion is that God broke the silence because a woman of prayer had made a sacrifice of her only son. It was not a sacrifice of merit—for God Himself had given her the child. She could not boast of "earning God's favor." But it was a sacrifice of "a broken and contrite heart"; the kind of sacrifice that most honors God's grace and mercy. Her son, Samuel, knew very well from his mother's own testimony that the Lord Almighty heard the prayers of His people. He therefore was ready to hear the Word of the Lord.

Do we daily wait upon the Lord, saying, "Speak, Lord, for Your servant is listening"? If God could say anything to you right now, what would He say? We spend hours listening to human analysis and opinion. We accumulate volumes of human writings. We invest significant sums of money pursuing human wisdom. What would happen if we spent one hour with the one Book that reveals the heart and mind of God? And what if the next generation saw that our choices, our values, and our priorities were based on biblical principles which may be out of step with the times, but are in step with eternity?

This is the seed that will bear fruit in the most barren circumstances. In another era, when the people of God were again desperate, the Lord invited their full dependence,

> Come, all you who are thirsty, come to the waters; and you who have no money, come, buy and eat! Come, buy wine and milk without money and without cost.... Seek the Lord while He may be found; call upon Him while He is near...As the rain and the snow come down from heaven, and do not return to it without watering the earth, and making it bud and flourish, so that it yields seed for the sower and bread for the eater, so is My Word that goes out from My mouth; It will not return to Me empty, but will accomplish what I desire and achieve the purpose for which I sent it.
>
> (Isa. 55:1, 6, 10-11)

Our dependence upon God is firmly grounded in the dependability of His Word. God's Word is a seed of irresistible power. As it is tilled into the soil of our lives, it bears fruit in the renewal of our mind, the awakening of our spirits, and the empowering of our discipleship. As we shape our worldview by the revelation of God instead of by the speculation of people, we see life clearly. We then are able to encourage ourselves and the upcoming generations with God's vision of hope, rooted in His eternal faithfulness.

The Seed of Confidence in God's Coming Kingdom

God has not withdrawn from history. His kingdom is coming and His will is being done. The fourth seed of hope is that which empowers people with the resources of God's Good News in Jesus Christ. Hannah's song of praise and prayer in 1 Samuel 2 describes God doing an even greater thing than giving her a son. God seems to have revealed to Hannah that a new era was dawning in the life of God's people. She prayed:

> My heart rejoices in the Lord;
>   in the Lord my horn is lifted high.
> My mouth boasts over my enemies,
>   for I delight in Your deliverance ...
> The Lord sends poverty and wealth;
>   He humbles and He exalts.
> He raises the poor from the dust
>   and lifts the needy from the ash heap;
> He seats them with princes
>   and has them inherit a throne of honor.
> For the foundations of the earth are the Lord's;
>   upon them He has set the world.
> He will guard the feet of his saints,
>   but the wicked will be silenced in darkness.
> It is not by strength that one prevails;
>   those who oppose the Lord will be shattered,
> He will thunder against them from heaven;
>   the Lord will judge the ends of the earth.
> He will give strength to His king
>   and exalt the horn of His anointed.
>   (1 Sam. 2:1, 7-11)

Hannah's personal experience of deliverance from barrenness is seen as a pattern for the deliverance which God will bring His people through a king. Up to this time in Israel, judges had ruled. Under Samuel, God would permit a king. Hannah's anticipation of a king and of a new and wonderful kingdom reminds me of our daily prayer, "Thy kingdom come, Thy will be done on earth as it is in heaven." Hannah lived in joy in spite of her trials because she saw that a kingdom was coming.

God's kingdom *is* coming! We too live in this promise. There are those in our own day who see the faint greening of the first buds of revival on the barren trees of our culture. In his book, *The Sense of His Presence: Experiencing Spiritual Regenesis*, David Mains describes eight primary characteristics of God's presence renewing His people. These include a renewal of worship and praise, an awakening of love and cooperation within the fragmented family of God, a hunger for prayer, and energy to serve the Lord's kingdom in creative ways. Mains has described how these signs are evident today, in growing numbers of congregations.

Sometimes in the study at home when I close my eyes in prayer, the outline of the map from the office desk returns to mind. Then it is as though, when I kneel to pray, I'm viewing all of North America, and my normal concern is intensified for this massive geographic area into which we broadcast each day of the week but Saturday.

Often I visualize dark, angry clouds hovering over much of our continent. Even so, I'm able to discern what appear to be tiny fires in various places. Unfortunately there aren't many, and they're widely separated. While some barely flicker, the last embers of a once-bright blaze, others still burn with great constancy. But the longer I pray, the more tiny flashes I'm able to find. This is not unlike observing the heavens at night; the longer one looks, the greater the number of stars which can be seen.

In my vision of this strategic part of earth, I'm aware

that these bright lights are churches where the life of Christ is manifested. "But can't there be more?" my heart whispers. Those threatening clouds will extinguish some of the weaker fires.

As if in response to my prayers, some flames actually leap up and burn more brightly—small in number, yes, but intense and pure. Alas, the adverse elements begin to move in concentration against them. Watching this dark power forming and knowing what is soon to be unleashed, I become discouraged. "Why even pray? These burning testimonies haven't a chance."

But wait! Beneath the onslaught of foul winds, sparks now dance out from the flames under attack. Here now, over there again, and then in new places they spring up. Defiantly the little fires seem to shout to the storms, "All your blustering will be counterproductive, utterly self-defeating, only fanning holy flames."

This imaginative development encourages my intercession. "More fires," I pray. "God, if we just had more fires—hundreds, thousands of them, even tens of thousands. With more fires, the possibility for holy flame in these lands becomes reachable." I strategize: "There need to be ignition points everywhere, each catching and spreading and feeding one another, so many there won't be enough clouds and contrary winds or hostile rains to extinguish all the blazing lights."

Then, as if in response to my thought, which hardly takes long enough time to be called a prayer, numbers of areas blaze brighter—more starlike points flame, north and south, east and west—further increasing my faith. "Look, it's happening, Lord!" I cry. "Please keep the miracle alive!"

"Come and pray with me," I call in my prayers to unseen friends—brothers and sisters. I don't know many of them by name, but I do know our hearts and minds are as one. "Do you see what I'm seeing?"

In my spirit I hear their voices join with mine; soon

their intercession can be observed. For the first time a concentration of flames combines with another nearby. The action is dramatic, lighting the area with intense heat. Cheers unite our prayer vigil. All of us are caught up with the intense work of intercession, and in some strange way we know that what's happening is fueled by a force totally beyond us.

I attempt to identify cities which might be involved. Denver. Minneapolis. Toronto. Isn't that Baltimore? This must be Phoenix down here. Oh, if only a true phoenix is alight—a flaming new spiritual life rising out of earlier ashes.

The warfare intensifies. A great hostile wind now whips and blows against an area representing several counties, and the strong fires burning there dim. But when the contrary force has spent itself, the incendiary fellowship flares again. Before long it is brighter than before and noticeably expanded.

With this, a turning point has been reached, a key defeat wielded against the haters of holy fire. And suddenly, as though a signal has been flashed, there is a dramatic acceleration of flame. New burning torches appear, brighter ones, everywhere on the continent— Canada, most of the States, even areas of Mexico.

I gasp, "Lord, another holy conflagration that won't burn out for years to come. O may it be so!"

The time is crucial. To insure victory, I and my prayer partners must stay at our prayer posts. "Before too long," I tell God, "it should all catch. It's going to be impossible to stop what's happening. Come now, you foul winds, blow some more! You only fan our flames!" And then—

Well, the phone rings.

Or someone opens the study door and says, "Dad, did you remember I need a ride to my lesson?"

Or I hear, "Sweetheart, can you please feed the dog tonight? I did it yesterday."

—And I'm back, back into the more immediate of the two worlds in which I live.

But I don't forget. I don't ever forget what I saw when my eyes were closed and I knelt over North America in my prayers. I cannot forget this vision of what still could be.[6]

More fires! We can plant the seeds of hope, calling upon God to equip us, empower us, and encourage our spirits. Perhaps this is another application of Paul's statement, "But where sin increased, grace increased all the more" (Rom. 5:20). We live in the hope, the certainty, that God's grace will triumph.

To be honest, these seeds cannot be guaranteed to bring a harvest in the first month, or in the first year, and maybe not even in the twenty-first year. But they are the most powerful and productive seeds known to humankind. If anything can bear fruit in the most barren, arid soil, these seeds can! As we consider our situation, we have three choices: we can give up in despair; we can give in to cynicism; or we can give ourselves away in the eternal hope of Jesus Christ. The first two responses will contribute nothing positive to relieve fear nor to empower change. For those with the courage of faith, however, giving ourselves away to those who follow will bear "fruit that will last" (John 15:16).

Let's reconsider the image of Howe and Strauss. Imagine coming to the beach at the end of a summer of wild goings-on. The beach crowd is still exhausted, the sand is still shopworn, hot, and full of debris—no place for walking barefoot. But then you catch a glimpse of a figure in the crowd. There's nothing special about the person's appearance, but people are gathering around. They are picking up the trash and clearing an area for a canopy to provide relief from the relentless sun. Suddenly, someone starts singing and more are attracted. Smiles are replacing vacant expressions. Hands are clapping, while others are joining the clean-up. Someone has brought a grill, and they are setting up a barbecue. Others are getting their picnic baskets and putting their food and beverages on a table for any who want them. Now, the sound of laughter mingles with singing. Heads are turning, and the word is traveling in waves over the sand, "They say they're starting a movement. They say we can do something about this mess. This much we know: their message of good news is starting to make a difference."

It will make a difference! May it start with us!

May-Lenny Weston

INVESTING IN YOUR "R & D"
QUESTIONS FOR REFLECTION AND DISCUSSION

1. How would you describe the generation of your youth (which may be now!)? How would your parents describe your generation? How do your perspectives differ? none

rebellion the same

2. How do you relate to the description of the "13ers" situation described by Howe and Strauss? How does this outlook affect your relationship with the next generation? revival

much guilt to be overcome - desire a among youth

3. Malachi 4:5-6 describes the time when the Lord "will turn the hearts of the fathers to their children, and the hearts of the children to their fathers, or else I will come and strike the land with a curse." a return to the values + GOD

   a. Do you think the order of "turning" (fathers or parents first, then children) is important? Why or why not? of parents

   b. How do you think cursing the land relates to the actions of parents and children? How did it relate in Genesis 3 and 4? Divorce reaps sin - death

in childrens lives - what we do for God affect them

4. The author wrote of "the seed of affirming and valuing life." What specific ways can you think of to affirm life for those younger than you? Accept + love them

where they're at - Speak Truth to them in ♡

5. In order to plant "the seed of dependence upon God," we need to be nurturing our own dependence. In what particular areas are you feeling a greater need to depend on the Lord?

TRUST HIM for my childrens souls.

6. Review again David Mains' prayer dialogue with the Lord. What happens to you as you read it? How can you communicate "the seed of confidence in God's coming kingdom" to the next generation?

through GOD is in control dance

Chapter Eight

The Fellowship
of the Undaunted

The Promised Land never looked very promising to the people of God. True, there were abundant pasture-lands that could nourish milk-producing herds of cattle. And yes, there were fertile valleys to allure innumerable honeybees to flowering trees and plants. But there were also current occupants who did not take kindly to the idea that a God they had never worshiped had deeded their land to a vagabond people escaping Egypt. They enjoyed their fertile land and worshiped their own gods. They were not about to give up without a fight. The reason it could be called the Promised Land, you see, was that the promise lay not in the land, but in the Lord of all lands, the God of Israel.

In our day, God's ideal for life, which is the Promised Land of Jesus' followers, does not look very promising. This ideal, which we call the kingdom of God, is not coming very rapidly. Yes, there are many good things which we experience because of our faith, but the world is in fierce opposition to us. In fact, many aspects of contemporary life indicate that the cause of Christ is losing the ground it had once held as a stronghold. Church attendance, for example, in England and Europe is consistently below 10 percent of their population. Additionally, the cause of Christ is not gaining ground in areas where we would expect it to flourish. The state of Washington in the

States has a church population of 3 percent! Ninety-seven percent of the people have no official church relationship. Even when we acknowledge that the Gospel is making marvelous strides in Asia and Africa, that does not lessen our concern over these other losses and trends.

In contrast, evil is making daily gains in its grotesque assault on life. The power of the media brings the horrors of world conflict into our living rooms and leaves us numb with that sense of responsibility where we have no power. The local news brings word of gun incidents on elementary school grounds, domestic violence, and desperate poverty. Human courtesy is a thing of the past. Manners are hardening with hearts as suspicion and fear fragment our social order. Random violence violates our insistent instinct to make sense of life. Its escalation suggests a frightening momentum as we project it into the future. Apocalyptic nightmares of a new Dark Age of tribulation are much less unreasonable than many had first thought.

The fear that evil is rising unchecked grips our hearts. This fear is perhaps the most difficult of all because we cannot attach it to a finite object, person, process, or event. It is a "free-floating" fear, feeding on threats which overwhelm us. It taunts us like night shadows as we strain the see the truth. Trying to resist it is like trying to punch your way through fog.

The ultimate fear is that evil will overpower the people of God. Will the church finally succumb to the relentless advance of foul forces? Will the sulphurous flames of falsehood consume the literature of Truth? Will the noise of evil calling to evil drown out the proclamation of the Gospel? Will the gags of respectability and "political correctness" silence the hard word of godly rebuke and correction? Will meaningless violence forever quench kindness between strangers? Will compassion freeze under the numbing chill of cruel assaults?

To help us gain perspective, we must realize that since the Garden of Eden, human history has been played out on the stage of moral (not simply mortal) combat between good and evil. We need to note from the start that good and evil are not equal but opposite forces. The concept of equality between good and evil, also known as "dualism," is not biblical. It derives from sources such as Zoroastrianism of ancient Persia, which taught that the universe is divided equally into two cosmic forces. The Bible clearly teaches that the Triune God, who is holy and very good, is the Creator of all and supreme over all. There was a time when there was no evil, and there will be a time when evil is judged and disposed of in accordance with God's will. In the present, however, good and evil are antagonistic forces locked in a wrestling match.

As we have seen in our consideration of the fear of aging, illness, and death, the Bible does not give a definitive explanation as to why evil exists. It focuses instead on our response to evil. The fact is, we live in an age of fear and evil. Therefore, our energies need to be devoted to learning how to respond when the power of evil seems to be gaining momentum. What do we do when our resources seem too puny, our thoughts too confused, our arguments too weak, our character too shaky, and our will too unstable to withstand evil's onslaught?

We can find help by looking at the "case studies" of people who've already been through this. God's folk have been on this road before. "No testing has overtaken you that is not common to everyone" (1 Cor. 10:13, NRSVB). Another passage states, "Resist [the devil], steadfast in your faith, for you know that your brothers and sisters in all the world are undergoing the same kinds of suffering" (1 Peter 5:9, NRSVB). We are not being asked to endure exceptional trials. We are being asked to be faithful in a rebel world. How we respond in our generation makes a difference to ourselves and to those who follow. In our fight against evil in our day, we join with God's people throughout the ages who have faced the giants who guard the gates of hell.

There Are Giants in the Land—Again!

The most common human response to overwhelming evil is vividly portrayed in the account of the spies who reconnoitered the Promised Land for Moses as the people of Israel camped east of the Jordan.

God had commanded the people to enter the land, but they

first wanted a reconnaissance mission (Deut. 1:22). The idea seemed good to Moses, so a representative from each tribe was chosen to explore the land.

At this point, there is a tension we must acknowledge: the tension between the value of human planning (such as sending the spies to look over the land) and the necessity of our full reliance upon the Lord. We cannot say one way is all right and the other all wrong. It would be as inaccurate to say that reliance on God negates human planning as it would be to say that human planning negates reliance on God. The Book of Proverbs frequently counsels us to seek wise advisers and to anticipate difficulties through careful preparation (see Prov. 20:18). In His Parable of the Tower, Jesus likewise affirms "counting the cost" before beginning a risky task (Luke 14:28-30). Human planning, however, is not sufficient. Our best plans amount to nothing apart from the guidance and provision of God. This is not an "either/or" situation; it is a "both/and" one.

In this case, the sending of spies seemed consistent with the obedience of faith. We need to beware of judging Moses harshly, as if God's command was not honored. Sending spies *per se*, need not have been a problem. The problem arose when the strategy of exploring the land became, not a means to accomplishing God's will, but an impediment and deterrent to doing it. Initially, the goal of the spies was not to determine whether or not they should enter the land, but the best way they should enter. The purpose changed, however, when their reconnaissance convinced most of them that the obstacles were too great.

The spies explored the land for forty days and found that the land indeed lived up to promises of God. But they were intimidated by the inhabitants. "We can't attack those people; they are stronger than we are" (Num. 13:31). As word of the spies spread, exaggeration fueled a wildfire of gossip until the people were ablaze with indignation and panic. "The land we explored devours those living in it. All the people there are of great size. We saw the Nephilim there (the descendants of Anak come from the Nephilim). We seemed like grasshoppers in our own eyes, and we looked the same to them" (v. 33).

This is the most common reaction to evil: we are not strong

enough. This is the flip side of exaggerating the power of evil; we minimize and devalue the power of good, of God, and of our own resources. This *intimidation reflex* blinds us to the resources we have in faith, while magnifying the opposition. If the spark of this fear catches in the kindling of unbelief, it ignites a fire which consumes all courage and resolve. We try to outrun the flames, but surrender all we value to the destruction we assume is inevitable.

This reflex not only empowers evil, but it also devalues God's mighty works in the past. This devaluing is seen in Israel's "Nostalgia of Unbelief." Following the spies account, the people began to complain that they had ever left Egypt (see Num. 14). They even wanted to choose leaders who would take them back to Egypt—back to the threat of infanticide for their male babies, back to degrading slavery, back to oppression, exploitation, and injustice! How could it be that the people would reinterpret Egypt as the "good ol' days" for Israel? The nostalgia of unbelief is evidence of the incredible power of fear to deceive the mind and distort the truth.

John Haggai, in his book, *Winning Over Pain, Fear, and Worry,* explains this phenomenon in terms of three levels of fear.[1] The first level is that of rational fear. In rational fear, the level of fear we experience is in proportion to the level of danger we confront. This is our God-given capacity for preservation in the face of threat. The second level of fear is "exaggerated fear" in which the fear response is out of proportion to the danger. This happens when our perception is distorted by factors like anxiety and bad information. We create what Haggai calls a "fear scenario" in which a sense of foreboding grows into a vivid anticipation or fantasy of future disaster. This exaggerated fear begins to interrupt our normal activities and control our decisions. The third, and worst, level of fear is "irrational fear" which is most often characterized as a phobia. At this point, a fear becomes the controlling factor in a person's life, robbing him of freedom and joy.

We can debate whether or not Israel was at level two or level three fear, but it is clear that exaggeration had won the day. The people were intimidated by the magnitude of evil. Panic overcame faith. Fear eclipsed obedience.

Paralyzed by the Intimidation Reflex

Information is a dangerous thing. Some say that information is power, but they forget to tell us that it can also be a liability. Knowledge usually comes with a heavy burden. As the spies learned about the Promised Land, they could not proceed with confidence. As we learn more about the evil affairs of the world, we can become overwhelmed, discouraged, intimidated. "Who is sufficient for these things?" we cry. For many, even those of the household of faith, the answer is, "No one."

For a while, it looked as if the United States of America was indeed a type of new Promised Land for the European settlers who came here. For nearly 200 years, the "Judeo-Christian" ethic (with a strong dash of "deism" thrown in!) helped define the nation's self-perception and policy. This nation did no` have a formally established religion, nor a "state church," but there was an informal religious establishment in partnership with government. All this changed when the social and cultural revolution of the 1960s sent shock waves through the entire national structure. The questioning of authority has led to a deep mistrust of institutions, including organized religion. The introduction of the birth control pill combined with the rejection of biblical standards for sexual conduct have redefined sexual and family relationships. The development of technological possibilities has far outpaced the development of ethical criteria for their application. In fact, the loss of the Bible as the primary reference point for ethics has left us with confusion and contradiction.

As followers of Jesus Christ, we are facing the Giant Secular. We are finding that our customary framework for understanding our ministry and our place in society is not working. Our relationship to the world has changed. Some say that we must once again view ourselves through the paradigm[2] (or worldview) of the early church. In his provocative study, *The Once and Future Church,* Loren Mead, who is founder and president of the Alban Institute, traces how the church has been dominated over the centuries by two paradigms: the "Apostolic Paradigm" and the "Christendom Paradigm." The apostolic paradigm describes the early church as a community of believers "called out" (*ekklesia*) from the world, living by the values of Jesus. The early church clearly understood that the world was hostile to what it stood for.[3] Therefore, the followers of Jesus viewed their life and mission from the perspective which I would call "realistic refugees." They knew they were not yet home. They were "an alien in a foreign land," to use the phrase of Moses in Exodus 2:22. They were not surprised by evil. They were neither naive nor indignant when the world "lived down" to their expectations, since they knew that apart from the arrival of God's kingdom, the world, the flesh, and the devil were dead-set against them. Their fellowship upheld the highest standards, membership was a rigorous process, and the commitment to their faith and to each other was vital.

Then came Emperor Constantine. When this Roman Emperor was converted to Christianity in A.D. 313, Christianity became the official religion of the Empire. The followers of Jesus were no longer under threat for their beliefs. They could move about freely and openly. But what looked like a blessing resulted in consequences which significantly altered the understanding and expression of faith and practice. As the government established Christianity as a state religion, many "converted" for the sake of appearances and advancement. A "citizen of a country" was equated with a "lay person of the church." Authentic faith was no longer a criteria for church membership. The fellowship became diluted. "The local incarnation of church stopped being a tight community of convinced, committed, embattled believers supporting each other within a hostile environment. Instead, it became a parish, comprising a geographic region and all the people in it."[4] The distinction arose between "nominal" (meaning "in name only") and genuine believers. This also led to confusion between worldly success and godly faithfulness, often resulting in the compromise or overthrow of kingdom-of-God values and standards.

For nearly 1,600 years, this "Christendom paradigm" characterized the Western world. Over the past 300 years, however, significant forces have led to the "secularizing" of the West. George Hunter III outlines six watershed events which have altered the perception of faith, religion, and the role of the church in society.⁵ First was the Renaissance. The rediscovery of ancient Greek philosophy, science, and literature redirected scholars' attention from focusing on God and theology to studies of human progress and the celebration of humanism. Second, the Reformation diluted the impact of the church as a social power, turning its energies inward, in an effort to recapture truth and integrity in matters of doctrine and practice. The disagreements among branches of Christendom caused people to question their loyalty to the faith altogether. Third, nationalism, primarily in Europe, resulted in unprecedented warfare between people who claimed, within their cultures and traditions, the Christian faith. The two world wars of the twentieth century generated doubt and disillusionment concerning the validity of Christian faith and the church. Fourth, the rise of science challenged the traditional Christian worldview. For example, Copernicus and Galileo demonstrated that the earth revolves around the sun, in direct contradiction to the church's teaching. The church's inability to distinguish its cultural assumptions from accurate biblical interpretation caused many to discredit the biblical record and the church which interpreted it. Fifth, the Enlightenment of the eighteenth century built on the momentum of the Renaissance. The principles of innate human goodness and the power of reason led to the concept of inevitable progress. "Natural religion" emerged, seen quite vividly in American authors such as Emerson and Thoreau. Finally, with the advent of the Industrial Revolution, urbanization replaced the agrarian lifestyle. When the people moved into the city, the city was slow to move with them. The forces of the city, such as the drive toward the impersonal, the frequent conflict of pluralistic viewpoints, and the loss of the extended family, have multiplied the impact of secularism.

The point of all this is that we are living in a different world from that of Constantine and the "Christendom paradigm." We are living in a post-Christian world. Today, Jesus' followers are forced to contend with antagonistic intellectual viewpoints, aggressive social forces, intense cultural diversity, and a spectrum of religious pluralism unlike any previous generation. The loss of a theological and moral consensus among those who claim to be Christians has greatly complicated the church's coordinated and effective response to the challenge of the secular. At the time when we most need unity, the people of God are being subjected to fragmenting forces which have distracted our attention and drained our energies.

Through these factors Giant Secular has spawned a brood of evil giants which threaten to block the coming kingdom of God. What are some of today's giants?

Perhaps the most wicked of all is one I call "Angry-Orphan," born of the collapse of the family unit. The loss of a place to belong has created a frightened, angry generation which is lost in everything from sexual confusion to substance abuse, from devastating alienation to the creation of surrogate families such as youth gangs.

The angry reaction against rejection, poverty, and injustice is seen most clearly in the epidemic of crime. We seem to be on the brink of a catastrophe unrivaled since the terror of the Black Plague in the Middle Ages. An article in *Business Week* reported on "The Economics of Crime" in the United States.[6] In 1992, 14 million serious crimes were reported to police—a number which many believe is significantly understated. The total impact of crime cannot be reduced to simple dollars. The human misery is beyond calculation. Nevertheless, there is an economic price tag estimated at $425 billion each year! This is derived from adding together a number of costs: $90 billion for the criminal justice system of police, courts, and prisons; $65 billion for private protection such as private guards and security systems; $50 billion for urban decay resultant from lost jobs and fleeing residents; $45 billion from property loss; $5 billion in medical care for crime victims; and $170 billion for "shattered lives," the economic value of lost and broken lives. This is a plague of incalculable proportions!

Time and space prohibit the enumeration of other giants, but a partial list would include the epidemic of sexual immorality through casual sex and cohabitation; the rise in the use of pornography, especially in videotapes; the depths of political corruption, fraud, and graft contaminating all levels of government; the spread of militant hate-groups, and persistent racism. I would also include the rise of New Age religions and cults. These are especially devastating because they deceive those who are seeking spiritual truth but are vulnerable because they have no biblical foundation or church experience. We could add many other trends, but the point is clear: We are facing a malevolent barrage of immense proportions. Are we to go forward into the battle for establishing God's rule, or will we cry out, "Those giants are too strong for us"?

Empowered by the Faith Response

Not everyone in Israel succumbed to the intimidation reflex. Caleb, one of the spies who is described as having "a different spirit," silenced the anxious crowd, saying,

> We should go up and take possession of the land, for we can certainly do it. . . . The land we passed through and explored is exceedingly good. If the Lord is pleased with us, He will lead us into that land, a land flowing with milk and honey, and will give it to us. Only do not rebel against the Lord. And do not be afraid of the people of the land, because we will swallow them up. Their protection is gone, but the Lord is with us. Do not be afraid of them (Num. 13:30; 14:7-9).

For the faithful, the rude awakening to evil can become a great awakening to grace. When Caleb asked, "Who is sufficient for these things?" he knew that the Lord was. The strongest faith has its eyes wide open to the realities of this world and its heart wide open to the reality of God's promise. The faith response awakens overcoming power. *Our confidence is determined not by the magnitude of the evil which threatens, but by the surpassing majesty of the Living Lord whom we trust.* This is where you find the courage to join the fellowship of the undaunted. Our realization of insufficiency makes us available to become vessels through which God can pour His grace and power into our lives and circumstances. We are no longer blinded by inattention to our problems nor by presumptuous assumptions concerning our abilities.

Caleb responded with faith in the face of fear because he followed the Lord wholeheartedly. He was not swayed by the popularity polls which gave the vote to the giants. He was the founder of the fellowship of the undaunted. To daunt is "to lessen the courage of, to tame or intimidate." The people were daunted by their observations of the Promised Land. Their reaction made God's Word a mockery. Caleb knew that God could accomplish more in a moment than anyone could do in a lifetime. Tame the promises of God? Absurd! Caleb knew that God's Word was more certain than any compilation of human opinions. Caleb knew that to stand with God was to stand in victory.

Our faith in the resurrected and Living Lord gives us grounds for confidence that far exceed what Caleb could have known. One of the most concise distillations of Jesus' nature and work is Revelation 1:17-18. John writes,

> When I saw Him, I fell at His feet as though dead. Then He placed His right hand on me and said: "Do not be afraid. I am the First and Last. I am the Living One; I was dead, and behold I am alive for ever and ever! And I hold the keys of death and Hades."

Christ is the First and the Last. Jesus is "firstborn" in terms of His position of authority in the universe (see Col. 1:15-20). Jesus is "firstborn" from the dead, the "firstfruits of redemption" and the promise of things to come. The fact that He is first and last means, among other affirmations, that evil is neither original, nor ultimate. Evil, suffering, and opposition to the Lord are allowed solely within the confines established by the Lord. We are not deceived by lies to the contrary. Since evil does not have the last word, fear does not have ultimate power over our lives.

Christ is the Living One. Fear is defeated in the Resurrection. Evil can rise no higher than the level of the empty tomb. We are assured of the ultimate vindication of the Lord and His people. In the meantime, we are empowered for the work of joining Christ in "taking captivity captive" (see Eph. 4:8). Jesus is the dynamic presence in the midst of our lives and circumstances. Jesus is not locked up in a museum of religious memories. He is alive! He holds the keys to death and Hades. Therefore, we do not fear those who can kill the body but not the soul (Matt 10:28). His power is beyond our calculation; beyond our imagination. When the stone is rolled away from the tomb of our limited concepts of God, our hearts are resurrected to the hope He has for us and for this world.

Storming the Gates of Evil's Domain

This vision of Jesus helps us understand the power of Jesus' teaching concerning the role of the church in the kingdom of God. I wrote earlier that the kingdom of God, which I sometimes refer to as "God's ideal for life," is the Promised Land of Jesus' followers. A proper understanding of the kingdom in relation to this world can inspire a Caleb-like response within us and our fellowships.

In Matthew 16, following Peter's confession that He is the Christ, Jesus says, "And I tell you that you are Peter, and on this rock I will build My church, and the gates of Hades will not overcome it" (Matt. 16:18). There has been significant debate over this verse. Does it refer to Peter as a person being the foundation of the church? This is the traditional interpretation of Roman Catholics. Or does it refer to Peter's confession of faith as the foundation of the church? This is the traditional Protestant interpretation. While it is clear that the Lord honors and affirms Peter, it is also clear that Peter's confession of faith is of the utmost importance.[7]

According to Jesus, the primary result of faith is victory in the conflict against evil. There are several interpretations of His phrase, "and the gates of Hades will not overcome it." The first is that the "gates of Hades" refer to the gates of death's domain. In this case, the reference would be foreshadowing the resurrection of Jesus. Death's power will be forever broken by the Son of God. Those who believe will not die but will have everlasting life. A second, and not contradictory, interpretation broadens the meaning of "gates" to indicate the boundaries of evil's domain in every form. The manifestations of death are seen in the everyday problems of life.

If we work with the broader meaning of this second definition, we begin to see the scope of Jesus' promise in confronting
evil. Jesus is promising that the people of God are able to go *on
the offensive* in His name. The gates of evil will not prove stronger than the assault of righteousness leveled against them. We
need to get a clear understanding of this image. Gates are defensive. They are meant to keep intruders out. The image here is
one of God's people rising up to overrun the dominion of darkness (Col. 1:13). We are storming the gates of hell. They are not
storming us. As Caleb told the Israelites, "Their protection is
gone, but the Lord is with us. Do not be afraid of them."

In Jesus Christ, we are to be ON THE OFFENSIVE! This is
not a way we normally view ourselves as God's people. We too
often think that we are on the defensive. Understand this and
meditate long and hard on this truth: we are not trying to keep
Satan out; we are part of God's invasion of this rebel world!

Jesus' Parable of the Strong Man develops this same theme.
Referring to His own mission of deliverance of those who are
demonized, Jesus says, "Or again, how can anyone enter a
strong man's house and carry off his possessions unless he first
ties up the strong man? Then he can rob his house" (Matt.
12:29). Jesus came to accomplish a divine plundering of the
strongholds of the evil one. Now we are part of His plundering, conquering army.

We followers of Jesus live in enemy territory. What difference does this make? It helps us to better understand the
nature of the battle. Like the early church, with the "apostolic
paradigm," we know we live in a hostile climate. We are not
surprised by evil in its manifold forms. We do not see the
people of God as losing ground. We are gaining ground in
Christ. This world is not "friendly territory," welcoming our
service, but unfriendly, resisting our service.

In his book, *Transforming Leadership*, Leighton Ford describes a period of time when the people of God appeared to
be on the brink of extinction.[8]

England in the 1700s had fallen into religious, moral,
and social decay. Voluntary societies had worked hard
to establish hospitals, to publicize the inhumane condi-

tions of the prisons, to legislate against alcohol, and
establish free schools for poor children. Hard-line law-
and-order advocates had sought to reduce crime by
increasing the threat of punishment. They made as
many as 160 offenses subject to the death penalty.
Scholarly books were written to defend Christianity,
yet little in the way of a profound moral change had
taken place. In 1738 one high-placed religious leader,
Bishop Secker, asserted that if the torrent of impiety
did not stop, it could become "absolutely fatal."

The historian and biographer Arnold Dallimore writes:

The successive failures of the several attempts to better
conditions simply proved that the nation's trouble lay
basically with the individual human heart and that the
"torrent of impiety" would flow until some power was
found that could stanch it at its source.

During the very months in which Bishop Secker
wrote his foreboding words, England was startled by
the sound of a voice. It was the voice of a preacher,
George Whitefield, a clergyman but twenty-two years
old, who was declaring the gospel in the pulpits of
London with such fervor and power, that no church
would hold the multitudes that flocked to hear.'

Before long the young Whitefield left the churches to go
into the open air. God moved in marvelous ways, stirring
widespread response to the preaching of Whitefield, John and
Charles Wesley, and others. Society was transformed as the
power of God overcame evil. The effect of this movement was
described by the historian J.R. Green:

A religious revival burst forth . . . which changed in a
few years the whole temper of English society. The
church was restored to life and activity. Religion carried to the hearts of the people a fresh spirit of moral
zeal, while it purified our literature and our manners. A
new philanthropy reformed our prisons, infused clem-

ency and wisdom into our penal laws, abolished the slave trade, and gave first impulse to popular education.[10]

When the Spirit of God moves through a responsive, expectant people, the world around them can be transformed. A deeply committed minority can bring extensive change. Sociologist Robert Bellah believes that 2 percent of any nation can change their society if they have a vision of what they would like to see.[11] This is a rallying call to the people of God. Our vision is to be shaped by the Spirit of God, not by the forecast of futurists. We do not assume that the world will be cooperative. We do assume, however, that the Lord wants to use the church to be a divine instrument to overcome evil with good.

Too often, however, the church has become an institution instead of a divine instrument. The church as an institution is preoccupied with self-preservation; the church as an instrument seeks to spend itself for the preservation of others. The church as an institution is concerned to possess power; the church as an instrument knows that God's power is to be given in service of others. The church as an institution is preoccupied with preserving tradition; the church as an instrument is prepared to launch out into the next adventure. The church as an institution relies on outward measurements of success; the church as an instrument is faithful to God, leaving the results to Him. Only the church as a divine instrument will be able to survive and overcome the rise of evil.

God is able to use us to slay giants. Remember, we serve the God who enabled a young lad to slay Goliath in a single stroke.

INVESTING IN YOUR "R & D"
QUESTIONS FOR REFLECTION AND DISCUSSION

1. What "giants" are in your life? In your community? *rebellion*

School – hurt & "goat" Christians in area

2. What is your most likely response to these giants? Are you more like Caleb and Joshua, or like the other spies and Israelites? Do you see God's vision for what can be done, or do you respond with the *intimidation reflex?*

3. The author spoke about the difference between the "apostolic paradigm" of the early church and the "Christendom paradigm" which followed.
   a. Describe the distinctive characteristics of each paradigm
   b. What were the advantages and disadvantages of each?
   c. The author expresses the viewpoint that we are shifting from the Christendom paradigm to a situation more like that of the early church. Do you agree or disagree? What implications does this have for our understanding of the rise of evil?

4. How does the principle that this world is "enemy territory" which is being reclaimed by the coming kingdom of God affect your expectations of our society?
   a. What are the areas of stress and tension in this view?
   b. What things can you do to take the offensive? *Jesus*
   c. Who do you really believe holds ultimate power? How does this affect your response to fear?

5. What specific steps can you take to cultivate a faith response to the rise of evil?

God is in control
Pollyanna   Be glad
look for good coming
expect good

Commencement

We've made it! We've traveled on a long journey through some of life's darker valleys. We've begun to see that fear, properly managed, can become a catalyst to faith. To be "scared to life" means that we tap the energy of fear as a motive for growth. Our vivid awareness of need becomes the incentive to explore how we can change ourselves and our situation.

We have considered eight specific fears, but we may not have touched on the particular fear that troubles your sleep or preoccupies your waking thoughts. We have not been able to delve into subjects such as the fear of being vulnerable, the fear of telling the truth, or even the common fear of public speaking. An in-depth study of each fear could consume volumes and volumes. But I would like to conclude with five principles that can help us overcome a variety of fears we have not specifically discussed.

First, bring your fear to the light. When we harbor fears within, we lose perspective and the fear gains more power.

Like fungus and mold, fear breeds in the damp darkness of secret anxiety. The sunlight of honest admission and loving dialogue saps fear of much of its influence. The therapeutic power may also flow through the ink of a pen or the clatter of a keyboard as you bring it to the surface through writing. This process of "naming the fear" gives us a more objective sense of the nature of our battle, as well as suggesting clues for victory. Learn to recognize the warning signs of withdrawal and denial so that you can face the fear before its power grows.

The second step in overcoming fear is exploring God's Word and the wisdom of others on the subject. Nearly every imaginable situation in life is dealt with in Scripture either by specific teaching or the experience of biblical characters. Ask God to lead you to His counsel from His Word and then start reading expectantly. The answer may not come right away, but countless testimonies, including my own, assure us that God will guide us with His Word. As James reminds us, "My brothers and sisters, whenever you face trials of any kind, consider it nothing but joy. . . . If any of you is lacking in wisdom, ask God, who gives to all generously and ungrudgingly, and *it will be given you*" (James 1:2, 5, NRSVB, emphasis added).

Seeking the wisdom of human counsel in books, from friends, or from the helping professions is also part of God's provision. Those who think they must solve their own problems, without "professional help," wouldn't think twice of trying to perform their own surgery! The care of the soul is a complex art, requiring a variety of means to deal with this wonderful, delicate, intricate dimension of human experience. Thank God for the multiple resources He has provided and tap as many as you need.

This will be combined with the third step of exploring the fear itself in order to expose the falsehood and faulty thinking which fuels it. One of the most practical exercises along these lines is to ask the simple question, "What am I telling myself that seems to be causing this fear?" For example, if you struggle with the fear of public speaking, what are you telling yourself? Are you comparing yourself to the best public speakers you know? If so, tell yourself they started out just like you did, but kept at it, improving over a long period of time. Are you telling yourself that the audience won't like you? What reason have you given them not to like you? If they are your friends or classmates, most likely they appreciate you and hope for the best for you. Besides, you might consider what you can include in your message that will help your listeners feel a positive connection with you. When we begin to understand the unstated, often subconscious, assumptions that comprise our self-talk, we can begin to expose falsehood and tell ourselves the truth.

A lesson in overcoming falsehood comes from the movie *The Wizard of Oz.* In this familar story, Dorothy is caught in a tornado and wakes up in "The Land of Oz," far from her home. Through many trials, she discovers that she must visit the Emerald City to learn from the Wizard how to get home. When Dorothy reaches the Emerald City, many obstacles continue to block her from seeing the Wizard. The persistence of Dorothy and her friends, however, finally brings them to the Wizard's chambers. There, they confront the ultimate intimidation: the huge face of the Wizard appearing in billowing clouds of smoke greets them indignantly. With a booming voice he demands to know why they would presume to enter his presence without permission. As Dorothy, the Lion, the Tin Man and the Scarecrow cower before this apparition, Dorothy's dog, Toto, trots over to a curtained booth. The others are curious and move over to investigate. Pulling back the curtain, they discover "the Wizard" is a mere mortal man working levers and speaking into a microphone in order to terrify and intimidate. In the end, he was more a bumbling coward than an awesome wizard.

Many of our fears are posturing wizards behind curtains, terrifying us with displays of power that are all show and no substance. The discipline to stop cowering and start considering them in the light of God's Word and through the leading of God's Spirit brings us freedom from their power. Then, like Dorothy, we may learn that the secret has been with us all the time.

The fourth step to overcoming fear is to develop a response plan based on God's perspective of the problem and then com-

mit to following it. This plan involves the discipline of thinking new thoughts and of practical action steps. Write out
thoughts similar to the themes that have been stated throughout these chapters. Agree to call a friend who understands
your situation when the fear becomes a significant struggle.
Have a reading plan for materials that reinforces positive
thinking and progress. In all of this, plan for small steps of
success instead of giant leaps and instant cures.

Fifth, pray. The most powerful catalyst to faith is honest
conversation with the Lord who loves us. God remembers that
we are dust. He knows the depth of our struggle and the
riches of the promises that are ours in Jesus Christ. He is the
Lord who says, "Fear not!"

I close now with the promise that has sustained me on
countless occasions:

> But now thus says the Lord, He who created you . . .
>   He who formed you. . . .
> "Fear not, for I have redeemed you;
>   I have called you by name, you are Mine.
> When you pass through the waters I will be with you;
>   and through rivers, they shall not overwhelm you;
>   when you walk through fire you shall not be burned,
>   and the flame shall not consume you.
> For I am the Lord your God,
>   the Holy One of Israel, your Savior . . .
>   you are precious in My eyes . . . and I love you . . .
> Fear not, for I am with you" (Isa. 43:1-5, RSV).

May it be so, O Lord. May it be so!

Notes

Introduction
1. Paul Lee Tan, *Encyclopedia of 7700 Illustrations* (Rockville, Md.: Assurance Publishers, 1979), #1662.
2. Denis Waitley, *Seeds of Greatness* (New York: Pocket Books, 1983), 33.
3. Ibid., 88.

Chapter 1
1. R.C. Sproul, *The Holiness of God* (Wheaton, Ill.: Tyndale House Publishers, Inc., 1985), 29.
2. *Pulpit Helps*, August 1980.
3. Sproul, *The Holiness of God*, 37. [R.C. Sproul was the first preacher to make this observation for me, when I was a student in his classes at College Hill Presbyterian Church, Cincinnati, Ohio.]
4. Unpublished letter. Quoted with permission.

Chapter 2
1. Secretary of State James A. Baker III, National Prayer Breakfast, February 1, 1990. Unpublished manuscript of his message.
2. Ibid.
3. Tim Hansel, *When I Relax I Feel Guilty* (Elgin, Ill.: David C. Cook, 1979), 12.
4. John Powell, S.J., *Why Am I Afraid to Tell You Who I Am?* (Niles, Ill.: Argus Communications, 1969), 38–39.

Chapter 3

1. Richard F. Lovelace, *Dynamics of Spiritual Life* (Downers Grove, Ill.: InterVarsity Press, 1979), 101.
2. *Our Daily Bread*, Radio Bible Class, Grand Rapids: January 10, year unknown.
3. H.A. Ironside, quoted in Paul Lee Tan, *Encyclopedia of 7700 Illustrations* (Rockville, Md.: Assurance Publishers, 1980), #2839.
4. Maxie Dunnam, *Alive in Christ* (Nashville: Abingdon Press, 1982), 87–88.
5. Charles Bracelen Flood, *Lee: The Last Years* (Boston: Houghton Mifflin Company, 1981).

Chapter 4

1. Denis Waitley, *Seeds of Greatness* (New York: Pocket Books, 1983), 25.
2. Ibid., 26.
3. Frederick Dale Bruner, *Matthew: The Churchbook, Volume 2* (Dallas: Word, 1990), 533.
4. Ibid., 534.
5. Ibid., 535.
6. Fenelon, *Let Go* (Springdale, Penn.: Whittaker House, 1973), 25–26.

Chapter 5

1. A.W. Tozer, *The Knowledge of the Holy* (New York: Harper & Row, 1961), 9. Emphasis added.
2. J.I. Packer, *Knowing God* (Downers Grove, Ill.: InterVarsity Press, 1973), 154.
3. Rev. Darrell Johnson, "No Need to Re-Imagine," a sermon tape dated 3/20/94.
4. Source Unknown.

Chapter 6

1. *Our Daily Bread*, 1994 Radio Bible Class, Grand Rapids: April 2, 1994.
2. J.I. Packer, *God's Words: Studies of Key Biblical Themes* (Downers Grove, Ill.: InterVarsity Press, 1981), 202.
3. Their story has also been written up in *Power for Living*, Scripture Press, January 23, 1994.
4. Jeremy Taylor, *The Rule and Exercises of Holy Living and the Rule and Exercises of Holy Dying* (Wilton, Conn.: Morehouse-Barlow Co., 1981), 55.
5. Ibid., 52.
6. Arthur John Gossip, "But When Life Tumbles in, What Then?" in *The Hero in Thy Soul* (Edinburgh: T. & T. Clark, 1950), 114.
7. Ibid., 116.

Chapter 7

1. Neil Howe and Bill Strauss, *13th Generation: Abort, Retry, Ignore, Fail?* (New York: Vintage Books, 1993), 1.
2. Ibid., 33.

3. Ibid., 96–97.

4. Bruce Thielemann Tape, "The Art of Illustration."

5. Joseph Bayly, from my personal notes of a message delivered at Camp of the Woods in Speculator, New York, August 1982.

6. David R. Mains, *The Sense of His Presence* (Waco, Texas: Word, 1988), 172–74.

Chapter 8

1. John Haggai, *Winning over Pain, Fear, and Worry* (New York: Inspirational Press, 1982), 194–216.

2. For further reference on the concept of paradigm, see Joel Arthur Baker, *Paradigms: The Business of Discovering the Future* (New York: Harper Collins Publishers, 1992), 31ff.

3. Loren B. Mead, *The Once and Future Church* (New York: The Alban Institute, 1991), 10–11.

4. Ibid., 15.

5. George G. Hunter III, *How to Reach Secular People* (Nashville: Abingdon Press, 1992), 26–29.

6. "The Economics of Crime," *Business Week*, 13 December 1993, 72–85.

7. Jesus' rebuke of Peter in Matthew 16:23 cautions us against emphasizing the person of Peter over his confession of faith.

8. Leighton Ford, *Transforming Leadership* (Downers Grove, Ill.: InterVarsity Press, 1991), 88–89.

9. Arnold A. Dallimore, *George Whitefield* (Edinburgh: Banner of Truth, 1979), 31; cited in Leighton Ford, *Transforming Leadership* (Downers Grove, Ill.: InterVarsity Press, 1991), 88–89.

10. Arnold A. Dallimore, *George Whitefield* (Edinburgh: Banner of Truth, 1979), 31; quoting J.R. Green, *A Short History of the English People* (New York: Harper, 1899), 736–37, cited in Leighton Ford, *Transforming Leadership* (Downers Grove, Ill.: InterVarsity Press, 1991), 88–89.

11. Robert Bellah, et al., *Habits of the Heart: Middle America Observed* (Berkeley: University of California Press, 1985), cited in Leighton Ford, *Transforming Leadership* (Downers Grove, Ill.: InterVarsity Press, 1991), 68.